NATIONAL REAL ESTATE LICENSE EXAM PREP

THE DEFINITIVE GUIDE TO ACING YOUR EXAM WITH STRUCTURED STUDY PLAN, PRACTICAL SCENARIOS, AND AUTHENTIC EXAM SIMULATION

INSIDER TIPS FOR A 98% SUCCESS RATE

ESTATE PREP FOUNDATION

Copyright 2024 by Estate Prep Foundation – All right reserved

DOWNLOAD YOUR FREE BONUS NOW!

We have some exclusive bonus materials for you as a way of saying thank you and to further enhance your experience. These extras include:

- **BONUS 1: Insider Tips And Strategies For Success**
- **BONUS 2: Advanced Memorization Strategies + Anxiety Management**
- **BONUS 3: Free Book: How To Start an Airbnb Business**

To claim these valuable resources go to:

https://micolipublishing.wixsite.com/realestate

TABLE OF CONTENT

CHAPTER 1 - INTRODUCTION

OVERVIEW OF CERTIFICATION BODIES

When commencing on the route to becoming a registered real estate agent, one must traverse the complexities of certifying bodies, which play an important role in the licensing process. These organizations, most notably PSI and Pearson VUE, serve as gatekeepers to the real estate profession, ensuring that only those who achieve the highest standards of knowledge and ethical practice are admitted. This chapter dives into the critical functions and contributions of these certifying bodies in the field of real estate licensing, emphasizing their relevance in ensuring the industry's integrity and professionalism.

State real estate commissions recognize and permit certification firms to offer licensure examinations, including PSI and Pearson VUE. These tests are an important phase in the certification process for real estate professionals, as they assess a candidate's mastery of a wide range of knowledge essential for effective practice in the area. The complexity and scope of these exams reflect the tremendous responsibility that real estate agents have in their professional operations, which range from managing transactions on clients' behalf to advising buyers and sellers on some of their most important financial decisions.

The Role of Certification Bodies

PSI and Pearson VUE provide the infrastructure for the standardized testing process, ensuring that candidates from several states are evaluated using consistent criteria. These organizations collaborate closely with real estate commissions and industry professionals to create and update tests that appropriately represent current laws, practices, and professional expectations. This partnership guarantees that the licensing procedure remains current and in line with changing industry standards and legal requirements.

These certification bodies' tests are administered with fairness, security, and accessibility in mind. PSI and Pearson VUE provide a regulated environment that maintains the integrity of the examination process via a network of testing facilities equipped with modern surveillance and security measures. This level of professionalism in exam administration is critical to maintaining the legitimacy of the licensing process, and thus the public's trust in licensed real estate professionals.

1. **PSI: Comprehensive Assessment Services**

PSI Services LLC offers testing and assessment services for a wide range of professional disciplines, including real estate. What distinguishes PSI is its customized approach to exam services, which include both computer-based and paper-and-pencil forms to satisfy various state regulations and candidate preferences. PSI's dedication to excellence is seen in its rigorous production of exam content, which includes subject matter experts to ensure that the exams are both tough and fair.

2. **Pearson VUE: Global Reach and Technological Innovation**

Pearson VUE stands out for its broad global network of testing facilities and innovative use of technology in the testing process. Pearson VUE, which specializes in computer-based testing, strives to make the exam process as seamless and efficient as possible for candidates worldwide. Its global presence ensures that candidates in varied regions receive the same high-quality testing services.

In addition to its technological prowess, Pearson VUE is well-known for its strong security procedures that protect exam results' integrity. This emphasis on security not only preserves the value of the real estate license, but also reassures the public about the competence and professionalism of licensed brokers.

The Significance of Certification Bodies

The certification bodies' responsibility goes beyond simply administering exams; they also play an important part in establishing the standard for admittance into the real estate sector. PSI and Pearson VUE contribute significantly to the development of a qualified and ethical real estate workforce by ensuring that licensure examinations are comprehensive, up to date, and fair. This, in turn, helps to improve the general health and stability of the real estate market, as well as the protection of consumers involved in real estate transactions.

Furthermore, the dynamic nature of the real estate business, with its ongoing regulatory and market changes, necessitates that the certification process be adaptable and forward-thinking. PSI and Pearson VUE ensure that new entrants to the industry are well-equipped to face the challenges and possibilities of the modern real estate landscape by updating exam content on a regular basis and implementing cutting-edge testing technologies.

The approach to becoming a licensed real estate agent is characterized by rigorous evaluation and preparation, with certification agencies PSI and Pearson VUE playing an important role. Their commitment to maintaining high levels of expertise and ethical practice through standardized testing is critical to the real estate industry's credibility and professionalism. As applicants prepare to face the challenges of the licensure exam, knowing the role and relevance of these certifying bodies is a critical step in their professional development. PSI and Pearson VUE help to produce a competent, ethical, and dynamic real estate workforce capable of servicing the needs of customers and the larger community with integrity and expertise by respecting the standards of fairness, security, and relevance in the certification process.

UNDERSTANDING THE FORMAT AND STRUCTURE OF THE EXAM

Understanding the format and organization of the real estate license exam is an important first step for applicants seeking to enter the real estate industry. This understanding not only helps to structure one's study strategy, but it also relieves much of the tension connected with the unknown aspects of the examination process. The real estate licensing exam is intended to completely assess a candidate's readiness to practice real estate in a certain jurisdiction. It explores a wide variety of subjects, including property law and ethical considerations in real estate transactions. This chapter digs into the complexities of the exam's format and organization, equipping students with the knowledge they need to overcome this key milestone in their professional career.

The Dual Structure of the Real Estate Licensing Exam
The real estate license test has two primary sections: the national portion and the state-specific piece. This structure represents real estate practice's dual character, which is controlled by both broad, universally applicable principles and state-specific laws and regulations.

1. **National Portion**: The national component of the exam covers a wide range of topics essential to the practice of real estate in the United States. Property ownership, land use restrictions, contracts, funding, and agency principles are only a few examples. The goal is to ensure that each candidate has a comprehensive understanding of the fundamental principles and processes that underpin the real estate profession.

2. **State-Specific Portion**: The state-specific part is adapted to the laws and regulations of the candidate's home state. This section of the exam may include state-specific legal concerns, property disclosures, landlord-tenant legislation, and details about state real estate commission procedures. This section's substance and emphasis might vary greatly from state to state, reflecting each jurisdiction's unique legal and regulatory environments.

Exam Format
The real estate license exam is primarily multiple-choice, designed to assess a candidate's knowledge and grasp of real estate principles and state-specific rules. Candidates are allotted a total of 90 minutes to 3 hours to finish the exam, necessitating effective time management and a systematic approach to answering questions.

- **Multiple-Choice Questions**: These questions are designed to evaluate a candidate's ability to apply information in practical, real-world situations. They may include direct questioning, situational analysis, and the identification of appropriate procedures or regulations for specific scenarios.

- **Question Structure**: The questions are designed to assess not only factual recall, but also critical thinking and the capacity to make sound decisions based on a given set of data. This structure guarantees that licensed real estate professionals are prepared to deal with the complexity and nuances of everyday real estate practice.

Understanding the exam's format and organization is critical for creating a successful study strategy. It is also important to participate in study groups or locate a study partner to discuss and review material, as explaining concepts to others is an effective method for cementing one's own understanding. Active learning practices, such as summarizing material in one's own words, making flashcards, and teaching concepts to others, have been proven to be more effective than passive study approaches like rereading or marking text.

The Role of Exam Preparation in Professional Success

Passing the real estate licensure exam is more than just a necessary step in becoming a real estate agent. It is a thorough evaluation of a candidate's ability to handle the considerable obligations that come with the profession. The exam's emphasis on both broad, universal concepts and specific, state-level rules guarantees that certified agents are adequately prepared to represent their clients successfully and ethically.

Furthermore, preparing for the exam itself provides an opportunity for professional development. It demands candidates to gain not only a thorough understanding of real estate practices and rules, but also vital professional abilities such as critical thinking, problem-solving, and time management.

The "EE" and "OR" Rule

The "OR" "EE" rule is a mnemonic that helps you understand and navigate the complexities of real estate transactions and relationships. It's a simple yet powerful tool for analyzing the dynamics between various parties involved in real estate transactions. This regulation is highlighted in the real estate licensing exam, emphasizing the need of understanding the legal complexities and duties of agency relationships.

At its foundation, the "OR" "EE" rule is about determining each party's participation in a real estate transaction. The suffix "OR" represents the party who is giving or providing something, whereas the suffix "EE" identifies the party receiving. Understanding this rule is critical for anyone joining the real estate industry, since it outlines the obligations and expectations associated with various real estate positions.

Application in Real Estate Transactions
1. Grantor (OR) and Grantee (EE):
- *Grantor*: The party that transfers property ownership – they are 'granting' the rights to another.
- *Grantee*: The recipient of the property rights or title.

This distinction is crucial in property sales, where clear understanding of each party's role ensures the smooth transfer of titles and rights.

2. Lessor (OR) and Lessee (EE):
- *Lessor*: The property owner who leases out the property – essentially 'lending' the use of the property.
- *Lessee*: The party taking the property on lease, receiving the right to use it under agreed terms.

The clarity provided by the "OR" "EE" rule in leasing agreements highlights the duties and rights of each party, critical for managing rental properties.

3. Optionor (OR) and Optionee (EE):
- *Optionor*: The seller who gives the buyer the option to purchase the property at a specific price within a set time frame.
- *Optionee*: The buyer is given the right or opportunity to acquire the property.

Understanding options and rights to purchase are advanced concepts covered in the real estate exam, essential for navigating investment and sales strategies.

Significance in Agency Relationships

Agency relationships in real estate define the fiduciary responsibilities between agents and their clients. The "OR" "EE" rule aids in distinguishing these roles:

- **Principal (OR)**: The client who authorizes an agent to act on their behalf in real estate transactions.
- **Agent (EE)**: The professional authorized to operate in the name of the principal.

Grasping this distinction is vital for real estate professionals, as it governs the ethical and legal framework within which they operate, ensuring they act in their clients' best interests.

The real estate license exam assesses candidates' comprehension of these principles, determining their ability to conduct real estate transactions responsibly and ethically. Mastery of the "OR" "EE" rule and its application to various scenarios demonstrates a candidate's ability to understand the legal complexity of real estate transactions and agency partnerships.

The "OR" "EE" rule is not just a mnemonic; it is a fundamental idea that influences our understanding of roles and duties in real estate transactions. Candidates studying for the real estate licensing exam should have a thorough understanding of this rule and its practical implementations. It not only helps them pass the exam, but it also prepares them for a successful career in real estate, guaranteeing they can properly manage the complexities of real estate transactions while adhering to the industry's standards of professionalism and ethics.

In summary, the real estate licensing exam is an important part of the real estate professional road, as it ensures that all practitioners have a high level of knowledge and ethical practice. Understanding the methodology and structure of the exam allows students to approach their preparation with confidence and clarity, building the groundwork for their future success in the profession. As a result, this chapter not only serves as a study guide for the exam, but also as an introduction to the lifelong learning and professional development that are essential for a successful real estate career.

CHAPTER 2 - REAL ESTATE OWNERSHIP AND PROPERTY RIGHTS

TYPES OF PROPERTY, OWNERSHIP AND TITLES

An accurate understanding of property kinds, ownership, and title concepts is the foundation of a successful profession and, more importantly, the real estate license exam. This chapter will analyze these fundamental concepts, providing a clear, systematic understanding that is essential for any aspiring real estate practitioner.

Types of Property: An Initial Overview
Understanding property types is essential in real estate practice and examination. This section briefly introduces the concepts of real and personal property as a precursor to more detailed exploration in subsequent chapters.

- **Real property** refers to land and its permanent attachments, including natural features like trees and water, as well as man-made structures like buildings and fences. Real property ownership is complex, having a variety of rights such as use, exclusion, and disposition.
- **Personal property** refers to mobile goods not permanently affixed to land. Personal property encompasses everything from cars and furnishings to stocks and other intangible assets. Recognizing the distinction between these two forms of property is crucial since each group is subject to various rules and procedures in real estate transactions.

Ownership and Its Intricacies
Real estate ownership is a complex term that encompasses a variety of legal definitions, rights, and structures that govern how property is kept, transferred, and used. This complex aspect of ownership is fundamental to the practice of real estate, influencing everything from transactional dynamics to property owners' legal obligations. In this in-depth examination, we will delve into the complexities of sole ownership, joint ownership, and common interest developments (CIDs), each indicating a distinct method in which property rights might be formed.

1. Sole Ownership
Sole ownership, often known as severally ownership, is the simplest straightforward type of property ownership. In this arrangement, a single individual or entity has complete authority over the property and its usage while adhering to the law. This type of ownership is distinguished by the unilateral ability to make decisions about the property, such as selling, leasing, or modifying it, without consulting or seeking approval from others.
Sole ownership has the advantage of simplifying decision-making and eliminating possible conflicts that can develop in co-owned structures. However, sole owners carry full financial responsibility for the property, including taxes, maintenance, and any obligations secured by it. Furthermore, in estate planning, single ownership means that the property is subject to probate, a time-consuming and expensive legal process for distributing the deceased's assets.

2. Joint Ownership

Joint ownership, by contrast, involves multiple parties sharing ownership rights in a property. This form of ownership is further subdivided into several categories, each with its implications for property rights, transferability, and survivorship.

- **Joint Tenancy with Right of Survivorship (JTWROS)**: In a joint tenancy, co-owners own an equal portion of the property, and when one joint tenant dies, their interest immediately goes to the other joint tenants. This right of survivorship avoids the probate process, making JTWROS a popular option among spouses and family members. However, any transaction involving the property requires the agreement of all joint tenants, which might complicate decision-making.
- **Tenancy in Common (TIC)**: Tenancy in common, different from joint tenancy, does not confer survivorship rights. Each tenant in common owns an individual, undivided interest in the property, which may be of varied size. When a tenant in common dies, their stake in the property is transferred to their estate in accordance with their will or state succession laws. TIC provides flexibility in ownership shares and inheritance, making it ideal for investment properties controlled by different parties.
- **Tenancy by the Entirety**: Available only to married couples in some states, this form of joint ownership includes rights of survivorship and provides protection from creditors, as the property cannot be seized to satisfy the debts of one spouse alone.

3. Common Interest Developments (CIDs)

Common Interest Developments are a type of communal ownership in which residents own individual units but share ownership of common features such as lobbies, gyms, and outdoor spaces. This category includes condominiums, cooperatives, and planned communities, each with its own ownership model.

- **Condominiums**: In a condominium, residents own their apartments entirely and have a proportional interest in the common areas. The condominium association, governed by a board of unit owners, manages the common areas and enforces the community's rules and bylaws.
- **Cooperatives (Co-ops)**: Cooperative ownership entails purchasing stock in a corporation that owns the property. Ownership of shares grants the right to occupy a specific unit and participate in the cooperative's governance. Unlike condominiums, co-op owners do not own their apartments outright but instead have a proprietary lease.
- **Planned Unit Developments (PUDs)**: PUDs are planned communities that may contain a mix of commercial, residential and recreational areas. Owners typically have individual title to their homes and lots, along with a shared interest in the development's common areas.

Understanding the various types of property ownership is crucial for real estate professionals, as these structures have a substantial impact on property rights, duties, and interest transfers. Mastery of these principles helps professionals to provide effective client advice, negotiate legal issues, and support successful real estate transactions. As the foundation of real estate practice, a thorough understanding of ownership complexities not only qualifies candidates for the licensure exam, but also for a successful career in the dynamic sector of real estate.

The Concept of Titles in Real Estate

The title denotes ownership of real estate. Unlike tangible deeds, which will be covered in a later chapter, a title is a conceptual legal status that indicates an individual's or entity's right to hold, use, or dispose of property. Titles play an important role in real estate transactions because they secure ownership and facilitate the lawful transfer of property rights.

- **Clear title** means the property is free of liens or encumbrances that could limit the owner's rights. Ensuring a clear title is critical in real estate transactions to safeguard both buyers and sellers.
- **Title Search**, a process to be explored further, is the method by which the history of a property is reviewed to confirm that the title is clear. This step is crucial for identifying any difficulties that might influence the transfer of ownership.

Implications for Real Estate Practice

Understanding the many forms of property, the subtleties of ownership, and the importance of titles is essential for any real estate practitioner. These principles not only serve as the foundation for many questions on the real estate licensing exam, but they also have an impact on daily practice in the industry. They influence how properties are advertised, marketed, sold, and transferred, emphasizing the need of a thorough understanding of these essential concepts. By establishing a solid foundation in knowing these critical factors, aspiring real estate professionals will be better prepared to navigate the market's intricacies and serve their clients with competence and integrity.

DIFFERENCE BETWEEN REAL AND PERSONAL PROPERTY

Understanding the many forms of property, the subtleties of ownership, and the importance of titles is essential for any real estate practitioner. These principles not only serve as the foundation for many questions on the real estate licensing exam, but they also have an impact on daily practice in the industry. They influence how properties are advertised, marketed, sold, and transferred, emphasizing the need of a thorough understanding of these essential concepts. By establishing a solid foundation in knowing these critical factors, aspiring real estate professionals will be better prepared to navigate the market's intricacies and serve their clients with competence and integrity.

The Essence of Real Property

Real property, in its broadest sense, includes land and all permanently connected to it. This comprises not only the ground, but also buildings, trees, minerals, bodies of water, and other immovable features. The legal notion of immovability applies to interests, benefits, and rights that are inextricably linked to land, such as leases, easements, and rights of way.

Ownership of real property gives a set of rights sometimes referred to as DEED: the rights to dispose of, enjoy, exclude others from, and utilize the property. These rights provide the owner extensive control over their land and its use, subject to zoning rules, environmental regulations, and other statutory restrictions.

The complexities of real property rights need extensive documentation and public recording to establish and safeguard ownership. Titles and deeds are examples of such documents, as they serve as tangible evidence of a person's rights to real property. Understanding these agreements and the legal processes underlying them is critical for any real estate agent.

The Nature of Personal Property

Personal property, commonly known as chattels, includes all items that are not considered real property. This category is distinguished by its mobility and comprises both tangible goods (furniture, automobiles, and technology) and intangible assets (stocks, bonds, and intellectual property).

Personal property is distinguished by its transferability, which eliminates the need for significant legal documents associated with real property. Sales and transfers of personal property are often simple, requiring only a bill of sale or a comparable document to complete the transfer of ownership.

Fixtures are an important subcategory of personal property—personal property that has been so fastened to real property that it is now considered part of it. The assessment of whether an object is a fixture (and hence real property) or personal property is based on various considerations, including the item's attachment technique, adaptability to the property, and the parties' intent. Understanding this distinction is critical in real estate transactions because it influences what is included in the sale of a property.

Implications in Real Estate Practice

The distinction between real and personal property has profound implications for real estate professionals. It affects many facets of their practice, including but not limited to:

- **Sales and Transactions**: Real estate transactions must account for both the actual and personal property being sold. Clearly distinguishing between the two is critical for drafting proper sales agreements and avoiding disagreements.
- **Taxation**: Real and personal property are often taxed differently. Property taxes are levied on real property based on its assessed value and renovations. Personal property taxes may apply to certain types of property, depending on the jurisdiction.
- **Financing and Mortgages**: A security interest in real property is often required by lenders as collateral for a mortgage. The differentiation between real and personal property is crucial in determining what assets may be used as collateral and how they are treated in the event of foreclosure.
- **Estate Planning and Inheritance**: Estate planning often involves different considerations for real and personal

property. Real property may be subject to specific laws regarding inheritance and transfer upon death, distinct from those governing personal property.

In conclusion, the distinction between real and personal property is important to real estate law and practice. For aspiring real estate professionals, a thorough understanding of these categories and their legal ramifications is critical. It influences every area of their work, from transaction execution to property-related advice for clients. Mastery of these concepts is required not only to pass the real estate licensing exam, but also for professional success and honesty.

ATTRIBUTES OF LAND AND LEGAL IDENTIFICATION

Understanding the characteristics of land and its legal identity is an essential component of real estate practice. This chapter examines the physical and legal qualities of land, which is unlike any other resource due to its immobility, indestructibility, and uniqueness. Each parcel of land on Earth is individual, with its own set of characteristics that influence its use, value, and legal standing. This conversation intends to provide prospective real estate professionals with the knowledge they need to negotiate these challenges, making them more prepared for both the real estate license exam and their future jobs.

The Physical Attributes of Land
Land possesses several inherent physical characteristics that significantly impact its use and value. These include:
- **Immobility**: One of the most fundamental attributes of land is its fixed location. Land, unlike personal property, cannot be relocated. This immobility affects many aspects of real estate, from zoning regulations to market demand.
- **Indestructibility**: Land is durable and cannot be destroyed. While structures built upon the land may deteriorate over time, the land itself remains. This permanence makes real estate a valuable long-term investment.
- **Uniqueness**: Also known as non-fungibility, every parcel of land is unique, with its combination of physical characteristics, location, and legal status. This uniqueness requires precise legal identification to distinguish one property from another.

Legal Identification of Land
The legal identification of land involves systems and documents that uniquely identify and describe a parcel of land. This identification is crucial for the transfer of ownership, land use planning, taxation, and legal disputes. The primary methods of legal identification include:
- **Legal Description**: A legal description is an exact way to describe a parcel of land in legal papers. Unlike a physical address, a legal description is intended to survive as long as the property itself does. The Rectangular Survey System (also known as the Public Land Survey System), the Metes and Bounds System, and the Lot and Block System are three common techniques of legal description. Each system has its own application, which is employed depending on the property's location and historical background.
- **Rectangular Survey System**: This system divides land into a grid of townships and ranges, identified by their distance north or south of a baseline and east or west of a principal meridian. It is commonly used in rural and undeveloped land areas.
- **Metes and Bounds System**: One of the oldest methods of land description, metes and bounds, uses natural landmarks and measurements (metes) to define the boundaries of a parcel of land (bounds). This system is often used where land was first settled and surveyed.
- **Lot and Block System**: Used primarily in residential, commercial, and urban areas, this system identifies land based on a recorded map (plat) of a subdivision, with individual lots and blocks numbered for identification.

Importance in Real Estate Practice
Understanding the physical attributes of land and the methods of its legal identification is indispensable for real estate professionals. This knowledge aids in:

- **Property Valuation**: The unique characteristics and location of a parcel of land directly influence its market value. Real estate professionals must be adept at assessing these factors to accurately value property for sales, purchases, and investment.
- **Land Use Planning**: Zoning laws and land use regulations are based on the physical attributes of land and its surroundings. Professionals in the field must navigate these regulations to advise clients on property development, use, and investment strategies.
- **Legal Disputes and Title Issues**: Precise legal identification is crucial in resolving disputes over property boundaries, ownership, and rights. Real estate professionals must ensure that legal descriptions are accurate and up-to-date to protect their clients' interests.

Conclusion

The characteristics of land and its legal identity serve as a key foundation for the profession of real estate. These notions not only support the value and usability of real estate as an asset, but they also have an impact on the legal, economic, and regulatory frameworks in which real estate professionals operate. Mastery of these areas is critical for aspiring real estate agents and brokers because it improves their ability to serve customers efficiently, make educated decisions, and thrive in the competitive real estate market. As a result, this chapter is an important part of the real estate licensing exam preparation process, ensuring that applicants are well-prepared to begin their professional path.

CHAPTER 3 - UTILIZATION OF LAND AND REGULATORY MEASURES

GOVERNMENT AUTHORITY OVER LAND

The interaction of political authority and land utilization is a fundamental aspect of real estate practice, encompassing a complicated web of regulations, rights, and duties that control how land can be utilized, developed, and conserved. This chapter delves into the various ways in which government authority affects land, shedding light on zoning laws, eminent domain, environmental regulations, and taxation—all of which are essential for anyone preparing for the real estate licensing exam or aspiring to be successful in the real estate industry.

1. Zoning Laws: The Blueprint of Land Utilization

Zoning regulations provide an important foundation for defining and controlling land use. These regulations, passed and enforced by municipal and county governments, are intended to divide a municipality into residential, commercial, industrial, and agricultural zones, defining the types of activity permitted in each zone. Zoning rules serve multiple purposes, including protecting property values, ensuring efficient resource use, and improving people' quality of life. To understand the complexity and significance of zoning rules for real estate professionals, a thorough examination of their components, ramifications, and issues is required.

Components of Zoning Laws

- **Land Use Classifications**: Zoning rules divide land into distinct groups, each with a designated legal use. Residential zones may be further subdivided into single-family or multi-family housing, whilst commercial zones may be designated for retail, office, or entertainment purposes. Industrial zones are for manufacturing or warehousing, whereas agricultural zones are for farming and allied activities.
- **Development Standards**: These standards govern the specifics of building and development within each zone, such as setbacks (the distance a structure must be from the property line), height restrictions, lot coverage limits (the amount of land that can be covered by buildings), and density requirements (the number of units allowed per acre). These guidelines ensure that development aligns with the community's vision and infrastructural capabilities.
- **Special Use Permits**: Zoning laws may allow for special use permits, which authorize uses not typically permitted within a zoning classification under certain conditions. This flexibility is crucial for accommodating

unique or beneficial land uses that don't fit neatly into existing categories.

Implications for Real Estate Practice
- **Property Valuation**: Zoning laws directly impact property values by dictating permissible uses. A parcel classified for commercial use, for example, may be worth more than one zoned for residential use because of the possibility for income generation.
- **Investment and Development Potential**: Real estate investors and developers must assess zoning regulations closely to determine the feasibility and profitability of potential projects. Understanding the permissible uses and restrictions of a zone is critical for forecasting the return on investment.
- **Navigating Zoning Challenges**: Professionals frequently face zoning issues, such as non-conforming uses (existing uses that do not comply with present zoning standards) or the requirement for variances (zoning exceptions). Successfully overcoming these issues necessitates a thorough awareness of local zoning rules and the procedures for requesting variances or rezoning.

Challenges and Considerations
- **Changing Zoning Laws**: Zoning ordinances are not static and can change in response to shifts in the community's needs, priorities, or vision for development. Real estate professionals must stay informed about potential zoning changes that could affect property uses and values.
- **Community Opposition**: Proposed developments, particularly those requiring rezoning or variances, may attract opposition from residents concerned about changes in the character of their neighborhood, increased traffic, or environmental consequences. Navigating community feelings and political landscapes is an essential skill for real estate agents.
- **Environmental and Sustainability Considerations**: Modern zoning regulations increasingly include environmental considerations, such as green space requirements, environmental impact studies, and sustainability criteria for new developments. Real estate professionals must grasp these criteria and how they apply to development initiatives.

2. Eminent Domain: The Power to Take

Eminent domain is a vital junction of public necessity and private property rights, with the government's capacity to take land for communal use emphasizing a fundamental component of land ownership. This power is based on the constitutional assurance that the expropriation is for public benefit and that the affected property owner receives fair recompense.

Eminent domain proceedings frequently include a thorough evaluation to determine the market value of the property in question, ensuring that the compensation offered accurately represents its worth. However, invoking this right might lead to disagreements about what constitutes "just compensation" and whether the intended use is truly public. Legal fights may arise, necessitating real estate experts' thorough awareness of eminent domain laws and property owners' rights.

Real estate agents and brokers must be able to recognize the signals that a property may be vulnerable to eminent domain proceedings, such as planned public projects nearby or changes in municipal development plans. Advising clients on the hazards, potential legal routes for fighting eminent domain proceedings, and compensation negotiation methods is critical to preserving their interests.

3. Environmental Regulations: Balancing Development and Preservation

Environmental rules are a comprehensive framework that aims to reduce the impact of human activities on the natural environment. These regulations address a variety of issues, including air and water pollution, wildlife habitat conservation, and hazardous material management. For real estate development, this frequently entails navigating a complicated approval procedure that may include environmental impact assessments (EIAs), adherence to specified construction techniques, and continuous compliance with regulations governing the operation of the completed development.

Environmental Impact Assessments (EIAs) are a critical component of the development process in many jurisdictions, requiring developers to identify and mitigate the environmental effects of proposed projects before receiving approval to proceed. This approach can reveal flaws that may necessitate considerable changes to project designs or result in the denial of development licenses.

Conservation easements are another method for balancing development and preservation. These legal agreements enable property owners to limit the kind of activities permitted on their land, frequently in exchange for tax breaks. These easements can be used to safeguard wildlife habitats, preserve open spaces, and restrict development in sensitive locations.

Green building standards, such as the Leadership in Energy and Environmental Design (LEED) accreditation, outline sustainable construction concepts. These rules promote energy conservation, waste reduction, and material and resource efficiency. Understanding and supporting green building principles can help real estate professionals comply with environmental standards while also increasing the marketability of their homes.

Real estate professionals play an important role in advising clients on how to navigate both eminent domain and environmental legislation, whether they are property owners facing potential land expropriation or developers looking to achieve an environmentally responsible project. Mastery of these complicated legal systems is crucial, reflecting real estate professionals' broader duties to their clients and the community.

4. Taxation: The Economic Implications of Land Ownership

Taxation has a significant impact on real estate decisions, influencing everything from property acquisition and sale to development and use. Property taxes, special assessments, and transfer taxes are all important components of the fiscal environment, and each has its own set of ramifications for property owners and real estate professionals. Understanding these factors is not only advantageous, but also necessary for individuals involved in real estate transactions, since they influence financial planning, investment strategy, and legal compliance.

Property Taxes: Funding Public Services through Land Ownership

Local governments impose property taxes depending on the property's estimated value, incorporating both the land and any additions, like buildings or other structures. Property taxes pay for the vast bulk of local services, like public education, and infrastructure maintenance.

The process of assessing property worth varies greatly between countries, but it usually entails a periodic evaluation of property values to ensure they represent current market conditions. Real estate professionals must be conversant with their local assessment procedure in order to provide correct advice to clients regarding potential property tax liabilities. Exemptions and abatements may be given to decrease the property tax burden for specific owners or types of property, such as homestead exemptions for principal residences, senior citizen discounts, or agricultural output incentives. Navigating these opportunities demands a thorough understanding of local tax rules and regulations.

Special Assessment Taxes: Financing Improvements that Benefit Property

Special assessment taxes are levied on properties that directly benefit from public works, such as the construction of roads, sidewalks, or sewer systems next to them. Unlike regular property taxes, which finance a wide range of services, special assessments are tied to specific projects and charged to property owners based on the estimated gain in property value as a result of the improvement.

Real estate professionals should be informed of ongoing and prospective public initiatives that may result in special assessments on properties, as these might have an impact on property prices and the attractiveness of specific regions for investment or development.

Transfer Taxes: The Cost of Changing Hands

Many states and localities charge transfer taxes on the transfer of property ownership, which are typically set as a percentage of the sale price. These taxes can be a considerable closing expense in real estate transactions, and they may be paid by the buyer, seller, or divided by both parties, depending on local custom and agreement.

Real estate professionals must understand the tax status. It allows them to provide full advise to customers, including tax considerations in transaction strategies, financial planning, and investment research. Tax rules and rates might vary in response to movements in government policy and economic conditions, necessitating constant education and awareness to maintain competency.

Furthermore, real estate professionals play an important role in lobbying for their clients, whether it's appealing property tax assessments, obtaining applicable exemptions and abatements, or determining who bears the burden of transfer taxes in a sale. Their skills can have a considerable impact on the financial consequences of real estate transactions, highlighting the importance of in-depth understanding in this field.

Conclusion

The government's authority over land includes a wide range of regulations and powers that have a direct impact on the real estate industry. The government shapes the real estate landscape in a variety of ways, including zoning laws that control land use, eminent domain rights that can change property ownership, environmental restrictions that safeguard our natural resources, and taxation policies that pay public services.

Mastery of governmental authority and its consequences for land use enables real estate professionals to efficiently negotiate the regulatory environment, advise clients confidently, and advocate for responsible land development and utilization. As such, this chapter is an essential component of the knowledge base required for success in the real estate business, emphasizing the interaction of government policy, land use, and real estate practice.

BUILDING REGULATIONS

In the complex world of real estate, building standards demonstrate society's dedication to safety, sustainability, and community welfare. These regulations, which are a complex mixture of norms and ordinances, play an important role in molding the built environment by impacting every aspect of building, renovation, and property development. This chapter delves deeply into construction rules in relation to land use and regulatory measures, with the goal of providing aspiring real estate professionals with the knowledge they need to navigate these legal landscapes.

The goal behind building laws is to safeguard the safety, health, and well-being of residents and the general public. These rules encompass a wide range of standards, including as structural integrity, fire safety, energy efficiency, and accessibility. They do not remain static; they change in reaction to technology breakthroughs, environmental difficulties, and shifting societal needs.

1. **Structural Integrity**: Structural integrity is a building's capacity to withstand its design weight without failing or collapsing. This basic part of building rules ensures that structures are planned and built to withstand not only the normal stresses of inhabitants and contents, but also environmental pressures such as wind, snow, earthquake, and flood threats. Building codes establish minimum requirements for materials, design processes, and building methods to ensure long-term durability and safety.

2. **Fire Safety**: Fire safety standards are essential components of building codes, meant to reduce the risk of fire and protect residents in the event of a fire. These regulations specify a variety of standards, such as the installation of smoke detectors and fire suppression systems, the use of fire-resistant construction materials, and the layout of escape routes and exits. Fire safety rules also specify the maximum occupancy for buildings and areas, ensuring that residents may evacuate swiftly and securely in an emergency.

3. **Energy Efficiency**: Building rules include energy efficiency criteria, which attempt to reduce buildings' environmental imprint by limiting energy usage. These regulations apply to many aspects of construction and building design, such as insulation, windows, lighting, and HVAC systems. Buildings that follow energy efficiency requirements can drastically reduce their energy expenses while also contributing to environmental sustainability.

4. **Accessibility**: Accessibility laws guarantee that buildings are useable and navigable for individuals with disabilities. These regulations, which are frequently included in broader construction codes, mandate public and commercial buildings to have wheelchair ramps, accessible facilities, and elevators. In residential buildings, accessibility issues can have an impact on the design of entrances, doors, and living areas.

Understanding and managing these parts of construction rules allows real estate professionals to better serve their customers by ensuring that properties are not only compliant with current laws, but also safe, efficient, and accessible. This information is essential not only for passing the real estate licensure exam, but also for helping to create excellent, sustainable, and inclusive built environments.

Building Codes: Ensuring Safety and Integrity through Standards
Building regulations specify and measure a building's safety, durability, and efficiency. These technical standards are rigorously established to handle all aspects of building, ensuring that constructions are not only safe but also resilient and long-lasting. Unlike zoning regulations, which affect the urban landscape by prescribing how property can be used, building codes concentrate on the specifics of construction, renovation, and building maintenance, offering a detailed blueprint for safe habitation.

Building codes include a wide range of restrictions designed to safeguard the public's health, welfare, and safety. These codes are dynamic, always evolving to reflect developments in construction technology, materials science, and safety research. Their scope encompasses, but is not limited to the following:

1. **Electrical Safety**: Building codes incorporate extensive regulations for electrical systems to guarantee that they are installed in a safe manner, reducing the danger of fires, shocks, and other hazards. These laws govern everything from the location of outlets and fixtures to the types and methods of wiring employed. They demand the use of ground fault circuit interrupters (GFCIs) in wet or damp places, specify service panel requirements, and detail the proper installation of lighting systems.

2. **Plumbing and Sanitation**: Plumbing requirements in building codes ensure that water supply, waste disposal, and drainage systems are safe, functional, and environmentally responsible. These guidelines cover water efficiency, preventing cross-contamination between drinking water and waste water, and properly venting sewer gasses. Regulations also stipulate the materials and methods for installing plumbing fixtures and piping in order to avoid leaks, blockages, and other problems that could endanger health or cause property damage.

3. **Ventilation and Air Quality**: Building rules also specify ventilation system criteria to provide proper airflow and indoor air quality. This comprises mechanical ventilation system standards for residential and commercial buildings, exhaust system installation criteria in pollutant-generating areas (such as kitchens and bathrooms), and energy recovery ventilation system use recommendations. These laws are necessary for limiting the accumulation of humidity, smells, and harmful gasses, therefore protecting tenant health and the building's structural integrity.

4. **Environmental Protection**: Aside from the direct influence on buildings, several construction rules are developed with environmental conservation in mind. These include erosion and sedimentation control methods during construction, stormwater management system regulations to prevent flooding and water pollution, and construction material sustainability norms.

Each of these parts of building regulations is critical to ensuring that construction projects achieve high levels of safety, functionality, and environmental stewardship. For aspiring real estate professionals, a thorough understanding of these areas is more than just passing the licensing exam; it's about ensuring the long-term safety, viability, and sustainability of the properties they'll work with, protecting their clients' investments and the community as a whole.

Navigating the Permit Process

The permit procedure is an important component of building rules, as it ensures compliance with zoning laws and building codes. Obtaining a construction permit usually entails submitting comprehensive designs and specifications for approval by local government officials or building inspectors. This procedure not only ensures regulatory compliance, but it also allows for easier control and inspection during construction to guarantee that authorized designs are followed. Delays or denials of permits can have a substantial influence on project timetables and costs, so real estate professionals must grasp the process. Familiarity with local regulations, as well as the capacity to negotiate bureaucratic procedures, is critical for good client advice and development project management.

Building rules are an essential component of real estate practice, as they embody the legal framework that governs land development and building. Real estate professionals may effectively traverse the regulatory landscape by thoroughly comprehending zoning laws, construction codes, the permit procedure, and environmental rules. This information not only prepares applicants for the real estate licensure exam, but also for a successful career in real estate, enabling them to advocate for safe, sustainable, and compliance development techniques. As a result, building laws are more than just legal obligations; they also provide possibilities to contribute to the establishment of excellent, livable environments in our communities.

SPECIAL TYPES OF LAND

The study of land in the context of real estate goes beyond residential and commercial properties to include special categories of property with distinct characteristics, uses, and regulatory needs. These specific property types include agricultural land, wetlands, brownfields, and greenfields, all of which create unique challenges for real estate professionals. This chapter looks into each of these categories, offering light on the regulatory measures, utilization issues, and possibilities they present, preparing candidates for the intricacies they will face on the real estate license exam and in their professional activity.

1. **Agricultural Land**: The US Department of Agriculture (USDA) manages programs and regulations that have a substantial impact on agricultural land usage. The Farm Bill, which is renewed every five years, covers a wide range of measures, such as crop insurance, conservation initiatives, and rural development. Real estate professionals should get acquainted with the Farm Bill's provisions, particularly those pertaining to conservation and land use, in order to advise clients on potential implications and possibilities. Furthermore, local zoning rules related to agricultural zones (A-Zones) specify allowable land uses, construction limits, and property tax assessments designed to encourage farming activities. Understanding these layers of regulation is critical for successfully managing, selling, or converting agricultural holdings.

2. **Wetlands**: The Clean Water Act (CWA), which is managed by the United States Environmental Protection Agency (EPA) and the Army Corps of Engineers, serves as the primary regulatory framework for wetlands. Section 404 of the Clean Water Act necessitates authorization to dump discarded or excavated material into US waters, which includes wetlands. Real estate professionals must be skilled at identifying possible wetland areas on a property and guiding clients through the Section 404 permitting process, which includes assessments of potential impacts and the development of mitigation solutions.

3. **Brownfields**: Brownfield redevelopment is heavily influenced by the Comprehensive Environmental Response, Compensation, and Liability Act (CERCLA), often known as Superfund. CERCLA establishes a federal framework for the cleaning of places affected by hazardous chemicals, pollutants, or contaminants. The EPA's Brownfields Program provides funds and technical help for brownfield assessment, cleanup, and restoration.

4. **Greenfields**: Greenfield development, while less constrained by historical use, must follow sustainable development principles and local comprehensive plans. Many communities implement comprehensive plans that lay out long-term development principles, land use objectives, and growth management measures. These plans frequently include explicit provisions for greenfield development, with the goal of balancing expansion, environmental conservation, infrastructure capacity, and community requirements.

As we close this chapter on specific forms of land, it is clear that real estate professionals' responsibilities extend beyond transactions and negotiations. It includes being land stewards, champions for sustainable development, and knowledgeable liaisons between regulatory frameworks and client interests. Future real estate agents and brokers must not only understand the complexities of agricultural, wetland, brownfield, and greenfield properties, but also use this knowledge to promote development that considers environmental constraints, community goals, and economic opportunities. Real estate professionals have a unique opportunity to define the future landscape by knowing the regulatory environment and strategic land use planning. This ensures that it is built on the principles of sustainability, accountability, and informed growth.

CHAPTER 4 - APPRAISAL AND DYNAMICS OF THE PROPERTY MARKET

PRINCIPLES OF VALUATION AND MARKET ANALYSIS

In the complex world of real estate, property valuation and market analysis are key pillars for making informed investment, selling, and purchasing decisions. This chapter digs into the fundamental principles of property valuation and market analysis, with the goal of providing future real estate professionals with the information they need to navigate and analyze the dynamic property market. This inquiry is about more than just studying for the real estate licensing exam; it's about establishing the groundwork for a successful career in real estate, where the ability to accurately appraise property worth and comprehend market dynamics is vital.

Understanding Property Valuation

Property valuation is the procedure of estimating the value of a property based on its attributes, location, and current market conditions. This process relies on several core principles:

- **Comparative Market Analysis (CMA)**: CMA compares the property in issue to similar homes that have recently sold in the same region. To calculate the projected market value of a property, differences in size, condition, location, and features are taken into account. The following chapter will go into greater detail about Comparative Market Analysis (CMA).

- **Income Capitalization Approach**: The Income Capitalization Approach is very beneficial when evaluating commercial properties including office buildings, retail spaces, and rental apartment complexes. This approach determines a property's worth based on the net income it is predicted to create over time, making it an indispensable tool for investors looking for income-producing properties. The process involves several key steps:
    1. *Estimating Potential Rental Income*: Starting with the gross potential income, this method accounts for vacancy rates and credit losses to estimate the effective gross income.
    2. *Calculating Operating Expenses*: Operating expenses, including maintenance, management fees, insurance, and taxes, are subtracted from the effective gross income to determine the net operating income (NOI).
    3. *Applying Capitalization Rate*: The NOI is then divided by the capitalization rate (cap rate), which reflects the investor's desired rate of return based on the perceived risk of the investment. The formula used is Value = NOI / Cap Rate.

This approach necessitates a thorough understanding of market rents, vacancy rates, operating expenses, and cap rates, which can vary significantly based on location, property type, and market conditions.

- **Cost Approach**: The Cost Approach is founded on the substitution principle, which argues that a prudent investor will not pay more for a property than it would cost to construct an equivalent structure from scratch, less depreciation. This strategy is especially useful for unusual or specialty properties with little comparable sales data, such as schools, churches, and government buildings. The steps involved include:
    1. *Estimating Land Value*: The value of the land as if it were vacant and available to be developed is assessed, providing the baseline for the property valuation.
    2. *Calculating Construction Costs*: This includes the current cost to construct the building and any other improvements, taking into account materials, labor, and builder's profit.
    3. *Accounting for Depreciation*: Depreciation reflects the loss in value from physical wear and tear, functional obsolescence (outdated design), and economic obsolescence (external factors leading to loss in value). The total depreciation is subtracted from the construction cost to adjust the property value.

Understanding the Cost Approach requires knowledge of construction costs, depreciation methods, and the ability to assess land value independently of existing structures.

Market Analysis Fundamentals

Market analysis involves examining the broader real estate market to understand trends, demand and supply dynamics, and factors influencing property values. Key components of a thorough market analysis include:

- **Demographic Analysis**: Understanding the characteristics of the population in a given area, including age, income levels, and population growth, can provide insights into housing demand and preferences.
- **Economic Indicators**: Economic conditions, employment rates, and interest rates all influence real estate market trends. For instance, a robust economy and low unemployment typically bolster housing demand, potentially driving up property values.
- **Government Policies and Regulations**: Zoning laws, tax policies, and land use regulations can significantly impact property values and market dynamics. Staying informed about local government activity is critical for reliable market analysis.

Applications in Real Estate Practice

The principles of valuation and market analysis are not merely theoretical; they have direct implications for real estate practice:

- **For Sellers**: Understanding how properties are valued and what factors are driving the market can help in setting competitive asking prices and devising effective selling strategies.
- **For Buyers**: Buyers can use valuation and market analysis to determine fair offer prices, negotiate effectively, and make informed investment decisions.
- **For Investors**: Market analysis is critical for identifying emerging trends, assessing the potential for return on investment, and mitigating risks.

The fundamentals of valuation and market analysis enable real estate professionals to confidently and precisely negotiate the complexity of the property market. Beyond facilitating transactions, these principles allow experts to help build dynamic, sustainable communities by ensuring that property valuations represent both existing reality and future potential. As the real estate sector evolves due to changes in technology, consumer tastes, and economic conditions, the requirement for skilled individuals capable of conducting valuation and market analysis will only increase. This chapter is thus more than just a basis for exam preparation; it is a call to future real estate professionals to recognize their role as major players in altering the market through informed, strategic analysis and action.

METHODS OF COMPARISON AND VALUATION

Understanding the methods of comparison and valuation becomes increasingly important as we progress into the field of real estate appraisal. This chapter concentrates on Comparative Market Analysis (CMA) while also discussing alternative valuation methods, providing a full understanding of how properties are valued in today's dynamic market. Through an academic viewpoint, we hope to provide future real estate professionals with the tools they need for accurate property valuation, which is critical to successful real estate transactions and market analysis.

Comparative Market Analysis (CMA)

The Comparative Market Analysis (CMA) is at the heart of real estate assessment; it compares a subject property to similar properties that have previously sold, are currently on the market, or have failed to sell. This study assists in determining a fair market value for the property in question by accounting for differences between the subject property and comparables (comps).

- **Selecting Comparables**: The selection of comparables is a critical step in conducting a CMA. Ideally, comps are:
    1. Geographically proximate to the subject property, preferably within the same neighborhood or community.
    2. Similar in key attributes such as size, age, condition, and style.
    3. Recent, reflecting current market conditions, with sales within the last 3 to 6 months being most relevant.
- **Adjustments**: The sale price of the similar properties is modified to allow for the differences between the comps and the specific property. These changes could include square footage, the number of bedrooms and bathrooms, lot size, distinctive features (e.g., swimming pools, solar panels), and the overall condition of the property.
- **Market Trends**: A full CMA takes into account broad market trends, such as supply and interest rates, demand dynamics and economic data that may influence property values. Understanding these trends is critical for

forecasting future market moves and appropriately pricing properties.

Other Valuation Methods
While the CMA is pivotal, other valuation methods also play a role in the comprehensive assessment of property value:

- **Income Approach**: Used primarily for investment properties, this method values a property based on the income it generates, capitalizing this income at a market-driven rate.
- **Cost Approach**: This approach (discuss in the previously chapter) is based on the principle of substitution, valuing a property as the cost of land plus construction costs, minus depreciation. It is especially suitable for new development and special-purpose homes.
- **Replacement Cost Method**: Similar to the cost technique, this method estimates the cost of replacing the property with a comparable one at current prices, which is important for insurance and tax purposes.

Real estate professionals must follow legal and ethical guidelines while conducting CMAs and other appraisals, ensuring that their analyses are unbiased, accurate, and reflect current market conditions. This includes following state and federal regulations, as well as recommendations established by professional bodies.

Valuation and comparison are more than just numerical research; they are about understanding the story each property tells and how it fits into the overall market narrative. For real estate professionals, learning these approaches is about more than just passing an exam; it's about giving actual value to customers and helping them through one of their most important transactions. As the real estate market evolves, the capacity to conduct precise, accurate CMAs and valuations will remain a cornerstone of professional competency, allowing practitioners to confidently and ethically negotiate the market's intricacies.

MARKET DYNAMICS: TRENDS, DEMAND, AND SUPPLY

The interplay of market dynamics such as trends, demand, and supply serves as the foundation of real estate economics, influencing every transaction from single-family house pricing to large-scale commercial complex development strategies. This chapter looks into these fundamental factors, providing an academic examination of how they interact to shape the real estate market. Understanding these dynamics is critical for real estate professionals looking to navigate the market's intricacies and help their clients make informed decisions.

Delving further into the mechanics of the real estate market necessitates a detailed grasp of how economic trends, sociological upheavals, and technological breakthroughs interact to influence both demand and supply, eventually influencing the property landscape.

Economic Trends
The link between the broader economy and the real estate market is undeniable. For instance:

- **GDP Growth Rates**: An expanding economy, indicated by rising GDP rates, typically boosts confidence among investors and consumers alike, leading to increased spending and investment in real estate. Conversely, a contracting economy can dampen this enthusiasm, leading to a decrease in real estate activity.
- **Unemployment Levels**: High unemployment rates can diminish purchasing power and consumer confidence, leading to decreased demand for real estate. In contrast, low unemployment levels boost economic optimism, encouraging more people to buy homes or invest in real estate.
- **Interest Rates**: The cost of borrowing is a significant factor in the real estate market. Lower rates of interest make mortgages more accessible, that boosts demand for real estate. Higher interest rates can have the opposite impact, slowing the market by making borrowing more expensive.

Societal Shifts
Societal trends extend beyond mere population statistics, influencing where and how people choose to live and work:

- **Urbanization**: The global trend towards urbanization has profound implications for real estate, driving demand in urban centers and potentially leading to the gentrification of previously overlooked areas.
- **Remote Work**: The COVID-19 pandemic has hastened the rise of remote employment, shifting demand away

from urban cores and into suburban and rural locations, where buyers can acquire more room for their money. This trend could reshape residential real estate patterns in the long term.

- **Changing Household Compositions**: Trends such as smaller household sizes, increased single-person households, and multi-generational living arrangements influence the types of properties in demand, from larger homes that can accommodate extended families to smaller, more manageable spaces for singles.

Technological Advancements

Technology not only changes how real estate transactions are conducted but also influences the very nature of property demand:

- **Proptech Innovations**: From virtual tours to blockchain-based transactions, technological innovations streamline the buying and selling process, expanding the reach of real estate markets and enhancing transparency.
- **Smart Buildings**: The demand for smart buildings, equipped with technology to enhance energy efficiency, security, and comfort, is on the rise. These properties often command a premium, reflecting the growing importance of technology in real estate valuation.
- **E-Commerce and Logistics**: The growth of e-commerce has spiked demand for logistics properties, such as warehouses and distribution centers, located in strategic areas that facilitate quick delivery times.

Market Dynamics: The Interplay of Factors

Understanding real estate market dynamics entails knowing how economic, societal, and technical elements interact. Real estate professionals must be skilled not just at understanding current trends, but also at forecasting future alterations that may effect demand and supply. This in-depth expertise enables experts to effectively advise customers, whether they're navigating the subtleties of the residential market or making smart decisions about commercial real estate investments.

Supply Side Dynamics

Land availability, zoning laws, and construction prices all have an impact on real estate supply. The development process itself, from planning approval to construction, can take several years, affecting the market's ability to respond to changes in demand quickly.

Zoning and Regulatory Factors

Zoning laws and building regulations play an important role in defining what can be constructed and where, influencing the supply of new homes. Changes in zoning regulations can create new places for growth or limit specific sorts of activities, dramatically altering market dynamics.

Construction Costs and Availability

The cost of construction materials and labor, as well as the availability of contractors and construction companies, can affect the supply side of the market. Rising costs can delay or halt projects, tightening supply and potentially driving up property prices.

In-Depth Market Analysis

To delve deeper into market analysis and forecasting in the real estate sector, consider how professionals use this information to navigate and predict market conditions, emphasizing the significance of a nuanced understanding of these elements for future real estate professionals.

Market analysis in real estate is a multidimensional process that combines quantitative data with qualitative insights to better comprehend the current situation and future possibilities of property markets. This process includes:

- *Historical Data Analysis*: Professionals examine past market performance, including price trends, sales volumes, and time on market, to identify patterns that may indicate future movements. This historical perspective helps in understanding how different factors like economic cycles, interest rate changes, and demographic shifts have influenced the market.
- *Current Market Conditions*: This involves assessing active listings, current demand levels, pricing strategies, and absorption rates. Real estate professionals use this data to gauge the market's health and competitiveness, identifying areas of opportunity or caution for their clients.
- *Economic Indicators*: Key economic indicators, such as consumer spending and manufacturing activity, provide

insights into the broader economic environment that affects real estate demand. Professionals must understand these metrics in order to forecast their impact on property values and investment prospects.

Forecasting Future Movements

Forecasting involves using the insights gathered from market analysis to predict future trends. This can include projecting price movements, identifying emerging markets or sectors, and anticipating changes in consumer behavior. Successful forecasting requires:

- *Analytical Models*: Professionals often use statistical models to forecast future market trends based on historical data and current indicators. These models can help predict price changes, rental yields, and market demand under various economic scenarios.
- *Expert Judgment*: Despite the availability of data and analytical tools, expert judgment plays a crucial role in forecasting. Professionals draw on their experience, knowledge of local markets, and understanding of industry cycles to make informed predictions.
- *Scenario Analysis*: Considering different future scenarios based on potential economic, political, or environmental changes allows professionals to advise clients on risk management and strategic planning.

Successful real estate experts excel at conducting detailed market study and accurate forecasts. It helps them to provide strategic guidance, make sound financial decisions, and confidently negotiate the complexity of the real estate market. As we move to the future, the real estate environment will likely adapt in response to changing economic situations, societal transformations, and technology breakthroughs. In this ever-changing climate, real estate professionals must have a thorough awareness of market dynamics as well as the ability to assess and forecast market moves in order to remain relevant and successful in the sector.

RECONCILIATION

In the complicated area of real estate assessment and market analysis, reconciliation is a vital last step in which an appraiser or real estate expert synthesizes information from numerous valuation methodologies to arrive at a final estimate of worth. This chapter digs into the concept of reconciliation in the assessment process, providing a thorough examination of its significance, techniques, and the careful considerations required to carry it out properly.

Reconciliation is the process by which appraisers evaluate and weigh the results of several valuation methods, like Income Capitalization Approach, the Cost Approach, and Sales Comparison Approach, to arrive at a single, conclusive property value. This approach is critical in ensuring that the final valuation opinion accurately reflects market realities and the property's intrinsic attributes.

To capture all of the features of a property, real estate appraisers frequently use multiple value approaches. Because of its specific focus and underlying assumptions, each technique may produce differing value estimations. Reconciliation entails closely examining the merits, shortcomings, and usefulness of each approach's findings in light of the subject property and current market conditions.

Reconciliation is fundamentally an exercise in professional judgment. Appraisers must examine the quality and quantity of data supporting each valuation method, the approaches' suitability for the type of property being valued, and the present economic climate. This procedure necessitates a thorough understanding of both the theoretical basis for valuation methods and practical market insights.

The Role of Professional Judgment: Beyond the Numbers

Professional judgment in reconciliation is about more than balancing numbers; it's about interpreting data within the context of a broader market and economic landscape. Appraisers consider several nuanced factors, such as:

- **Market Trends**: Current and anticipated market trends can significantly influence which valuation method is most reflective of true market value. For instance, in a rapidly appreciating market, the sales comparison approach might carry more weight due to its reflection of current market transactions.
- **Property Specifics**: A property's distinctive traits, such as historical significance, location uniqueness, or exceptional amenities, might influence its value. Appraisers must decide how these factors influence the overall

property value and which valuation method best accounts for these unique attributes.

- **Data Reliability**: The availability and reliability of data underpinning each valuation method are critically assessed. An appraiser must consider the source, recency, and relevance of the data used in their analysis, preferring methods supported by the most robust and applicable data.

Reconciliation takes place within a framework of ethical principles that require transparency, objectivity, and attentiveness. Appraisers must approach this procedure with a firm determination to produce an unbiased and accurate appraisal devoid of outside influences or conflicts of interest. This ethical obligation assures that the reconciliation process protects the appraisal profession's integrity and the faith put in it by clients and the market as a whole.

In actuality, reconciliation is more than just a theoretical exercise; it has immediate consequences for real estate transactions, finance, taxation, and investment analysis. Real estate experts must properly communicate the reasons for their reconciled value estimations, giving clients comprehensive insights into their properties' market stance.

The ability to reconcile is a critical component of real estate appraisal knowledge. It combines the analytical rigor of valuation methodologies with a deep grasp of market dynamics and property details, all within an ethical framework of accuracy and integrity. For aspiring real estate professionals, mastering reconciliation is more than just a prerequisite for passing the licensing exam; it's a lifelong skill that improves their ability to provide value to clients, navigate the complexities of the real estate market, and contribute to the profession's esteemed tradition of trust and excellence.

CHAPTER 5 - FINANCING AND MORTGAGES

PRINCIPLES OF REAL ESTATE FINANCING

Real estate financing is a key component of the property market, supporting transactions in the residential, commercial, and investment sectors. At its most basic, real estate finance entails obtaining the capital required to purchase or invest in property, which is often accomplished through the use of a mortgage or loan. This financing can come from a variety of sources, credit unions, banks, government programs and private lenders,   all with different terms, interest rates, and limits. The delicate dance of obtaining financing is a critical step in property acquisition, influencing not just individual purchasing decisions but also the overall real estate market dynamics.

The role of financing in the real estate market cannot be emphasized. It acts as the lifeblood of transactions, giving purchasers the leverage they need to make large investments in property. From a macroeconomic standpoint, the availability and cost of financing have a direct impact on the state of the real estate market. When financing is easily available and interest rates are low, market activity typically rises, with more buyers entering the market and driving up property values. Conversely, when financing becomes scarce or prohibitively expensive due to high interest rates, market activity can stall dramatically, resulting in stagnation or even falls in property prices.

Furthermore, the real estate finance climate reflects overall economic conditions. National economic policies and global financial trends both have an impact on interest rates, which are an important component of loan expenses. These rates can fluctuate in response to inflation, economic growth, and central bank monetary policy actions. As such, the state of real estate financing provides insights into national and global economic health, with ramifications for investors, developers, and consumers.

Real estate finance is also important for accumulating personal wealth. For many individuals and families, owning real estate is the most major investment they will make, typically serving as the principal vehicle for long-term wealth accumulation. The ability to finance property acquisitions enables individuals to participate in real estate with low initial capital outlays, leveraging borrowed funds to achieve ownership of properties that may increase in value. Furthermore, scheduled mortgage repayment promotes disciplined saving and investing, which contributes to long-term financial stability and asset growth.

In conclusion, real estate financing is a complex but critical component of the property market, influencing individual purchasing decisions, market dynamics, and broader economic trends. Its relevance goes beyond transactional requirement, affecting wealth accumulation, economic growth, and financial stability. As a result, aspiring real estate professionals must have a deep understanding of real estate financing principles in order to successfully navigate the market's intricacies and advise clients.

As we go deeper into the principles of real estate financing, we come across a number of phrases and concepts that are critical to understanding how properties are purchased, sold, and invested in. The terms mortgage, interest, and principle are key to this topic, as they all play important roles in the financing process.

Key Financing Terms
- **Mortgage**: A mortgage is a kind of financing designed primarily for the purchase of real estate. In a mortgage arrangement, the buyer (borrower) agrees to repay the borrowed funds, plus interest, over a defined time period, often 15 to 30 years. The property itself constitutes a guarantee for the mortgage, which means that if the buyer stops to make payments, the lender can repossess on the property to recoup the remaining debt.
- **Interest**: Interest is the expense of borrowing money and normally expressed as a percentage of the principal amount of the loan. The interest rate fluctuates substantially based on the borrower's creditworthiness, loan type, and current economic conditions. Interest rates can be fixed, remaining constant throughout the loan's life, or variable, fluctuating at regular intervals based on market conditions.
- **Principal**: The principal is the initial amount borrowed in a loan. Over the course of the mortgage, a portion of each payment is applied to the principal and the remainder is utilized to pay the interest. Payments are initially highly weighted toward interest, but as time passes, a bigger amount of each payment is allocated to lowering the principal sum.

Parties Involved in Real Estate Financing
The real estate financing process typically involves several key players, each with distinct roles and responsibilities:
- **Borrowers**: Individuals or entities seeking to purchase property who apply for and receive a loan under agreed-upon terms. Borrowers are accountable for making regular payments to return the borrowed funds plus interest.
- **Lenders**: Banks, credit unions, and private lenders are examples of financial institutions that provide mortgage financing. Lenders assess the borrower's creditworthiness, set the terms of the loan, and receive payments. They bear the risk if the borrower defaults but hold the property as collateral.
- **Guarantors**: In some cases, especially when the borrower may not have sufficient credit history or income to satisfy the lender's requirements, a third party might guarantee the loan. A guarantor agrees to complete the loan obligations if the borrower defaults, giving the lender more security.

Understanding the fundamentals of real estate financing, including key words and roles of the parties involved, is essential for anybody entering the real estate industry. This understanding not only helps you navigate the complexity of purchasing and selling property, but it also allows you to successfully advise clients on their financing alternatives. As real estate markets change and new financing options arise, maintaining current on these fundamentals remains a cornerstone of professional competency and client service in real estate.

Prequalification vs. Pre-approval
In the journey toward purchasing a home, prospective buyers will encounter the steps of prequalification and pre-approval for a mortgage. While often used interchangeably in casual conversation, these terms represent distinct phases in the financing process, each with its significance and requirements.

Definitions and Differences
- **Prequalification** is the primary stage in the mortgage procedure. It gives an estimate of how much a lender could be willing to lend based on the borrower's basic financial information. This stage involves minimal documentation and is frequently completed online or over the phone. The lender will inquire about the borrower's income, assets, debts, and potentially credit score, but none of this information is confirmed during the prequalification process. Prequalification gives an estimate of the loan amount but is not legally enforceable, thus it does not guarantee loan acceptance or terms.
- **Pre-approval** is a thorough process that accurately assesses a borrower's purchasing ability. During pre-approval, the lender thoroughly examines the borrower's financial situation, including credit history, income, debts, and assets. Tax returns, pay stubs, and bank statements are all essential documents for this procedure. The lender then sends the borrower a pre-approved letter outlining the particular loan amount, loan type, and interest rate for which they qualify, subject to final loan approval. This letter is normally valid for 60-90 days.

The Process and Information Required

The prequalification procedure is straightforward and quick, generally lasting only a few minutes. Borrowers offer a financial overview, and lenders use this information to determine how much they may lend. It's an informal approach with no expense or commitment from either party.

The pre-approval process is more extensive, and consumers must complete a mortgage application. Lenders then conduct a thorough investigation into the borrower's credit history and review the financial evidence given. This stage may incur a fee, but it results in a conditional commitment to the loan amount, which gives purchasers a competitive advantage in the home market.

Prequalification and pre-approval are both important steps in the home-buying process, but at distinct stages:

- **Prequalification** helps buyers get an idea of their budget, allowing them to look for homes within their price range. It's a quick way to start the home-buying process, particularly useful for first-time buyers to understand their financial standing.
- **Pre-approval** takes it a step further by providing a specific loan amount the buyer is likely to receive, making it a powerful tool in competitive markets. A pre-approval letter indicates to sellers that the buyer is serious and has the necessary funds to finish the transaction, potentially making their offer more appealing than others.

Understanding Credit Scoring

A credit score is a numerical expression derived from an analysis of an individual's credit files that represents that individual's creditworthiness. In the context of real estate financing, lenders utilize credit scores to assess the risk of lending money to borrowers for property purchases. Higher scores indicate reduced risk, which may qualify applicants for advantageous conditions for loans, like lower interest rates and down payments. In contrast, worse grades may result in more expensive interest rates or possibly loan denials.

Several key factors contribute to an individual's credit score, each varying in impact:

1. **Payment History**: Timeliness in paying bills and debts significantly influences credit scores, with late payments detrimentally affecting scores.
2. **Credit Utilization**: The proportion of current revolving debt (such as credit card balances) to total available credit. Lower utilization rates are beneficial.
3. **Length of Credit History**: Longer credit histories tend to boost scores since they provide more information on borrowing and repayment habits.
4. **New Credit**: The number of new credit accounts and recent inquiries into one's credit. Frequent inquiries or new account openings can signal increased risk.
5. **Types of Credit Used**: A variety of credit kinds (e.g., mortgages, car loans, credit cards) can boost credit scores by displaying the borrower's capacity to manage many credit products.

Lenders use credit scores as a deciding element in lending decisions. Loan applications are approved or declined depending on scores, which also affect loan terms. Lenders may set credit score limitations below which loan terms are less favorable or loans are not available. In this approach, credit scores have a direct impact on borrowers' capacity to obtain financing and the affordability of real estate acquisitions.

Role of Down Payments

The down payment is another important aspect of real estate finance, influencing loan terms, interest rates, and the need for private mortgage insurance.

A down payment is the original, upfront percentage of the purchase price paid by the buyer using their own finances and not financed through a mortgage. Down payments reduce the lender's risk by lowering the loan-to-value ratio (LTV) and guaranteeing the borrower has a considerable financial investment in the property. Larger down payments can result in better loan terms, including lower interest rates and the elimination of private mortgage insurance (PMI).

Common Requirements and Accumulation Strategies

Down payment requirements vary by loan type and lender, with traditional mortgages typically requiring 20% of the home's purchase price to avoid PMI. Government-backed loans, such as FHA loans, can need as little as 3.5% down.

To accumulate the necessary funds for a down payment, borrowers can employ various strategies, including:

- **Savings Plans**: Setting aside a portion of income regularly into a high-yield savings account or investment fund designated for the down payment.

- **Down Payment Assistance Programs**: Many state and local governments, and also non-profit organizations, give help to first-time or low-income buyers for down payments.
- **Gifts or Loans from Family**: Some borrowers may receive financial gifts or loans from family members to help cover down payment costs, subject to lender guidelines on such contributions.

Government-Backed vs. Conventional Loans

Understanding the difference between government-backed and conventional loans in real estate finance is critical for both borrowers and real estate agents. This knowledge not only helps borrowers navigate the various financing options available, but also matches them with loan packages that are most suited to their requirements and circumstances. Let's look at the distinctions between these two basic loan categories, including qualifying conditions and significant attributes.

Government-Backed Loans

Government-backed loans are distinguished by the support of a federal agency, which guarantees the loan, reducing the risk for lenders and often making it easier for borrowers to qualify. These loans are designed to promote homeownership among specific groups of buyers or in certain areas.

- **FHA Loans**: The Federal Housing Administration (FHA) insures FHA loans, which are renowned for their lower down payment requirements (as low as 3.5%) and more lenient credit score criteria. These loans are accessible to a broad range of borrowers, including first-time homebuyers and those with less-than-perfect credit.
- **VA Loans**: The United States Department of Veterans Affairs (VA) backs VA loans, which provide exceptional benefits to veterans, active-duty military members, and select members of the National Guard and Reserve. VA loans are noteworthy for demanding no down payment and no private mortgage insurance (PMI), as well as offering competitive interest rates.
- **USDA Loans**: Loans funded by the United States Department of Agriculture (USDA) aim to promote rural homeownership by providing eligible rural and suburban purchasers with 100% financing (no down payment). These loans are designed at low- to moderate-income people living in selected rural areas.

Conventional Loans

Conventional loans, on the opposite hand, are not guaranteed or regulated by any government body and comprise the vast majority of the mortgage market. These loans are often made possible by private lenders such as credit unions, banks and mortgage firms.

- **Eligibility Requirements**: Conventional loans typically have tougher qualifying conditions than government-backed loans, such as higher credit score requirements and lower debt-to-income (DTI) ratios. Borrowers generally need to put down at least 5% of the home's purchase price, though a 20% down payment is preferred to avoid the need for PMI.
- **Characteristics**: These loans offer a wide range of options in terms of loan terms, from 10 to 30 years, and can be used to purchase various types of properties, including primary residences, second homes, and investment properties. Conventional loans also include both fixed and adjustable interest rates.

A variety of criteria influence the decision between a government-backed and conventional loan, including the borrower's financial circumstances, military service status, credit score, and the location of the property. A thorough understanding of various loan types allows real estate professionals to better lead clients through the financing maze, ensuring that purchasers are well-informed and prepared to make decisions that match with their homeownership aspirations and financial realities. By demystifying the complexity of real estate financing, professionals may increase their service value while also supporting successful transactions and contributing to the general health and accessibility of the housing market.

MORTGAGE INTEREST AND HOW TO CALCULATE IT

Mortgage interest is the cost of borrowing money to purchase a house. When a lender makes a mortgage loan, they charge interest, which is the cost the borrower pays for the privilege of using the lender's funds to purchase real estate. This interest is often calculated as an annual percentage of the loan balance. Understanding mortgage interest is important in real estate financing for several reasons. First, the interest rate has a significant effect on the overall price of acquiring a home. Over the course of a mortgage, which can last up to 30 years or more, the amount of interest paid can exceed the original loan amount, considerably altering the affordability and financial feasibility of a purchase. Furthermore, mortgage interest rates vary substantially depending on borrower creditworthiness, market conditions and other factors. A favorable interest rate might generate in significant savings for the borrower.

Understanding the financial mechanics of buying and owning real estate begins with understanding how mortgage interest works. Mortgage payments are made up of two basic components: principle, which reduces the loan balance, and interest, which is the cost of borrowing the principal amount.

Types of Interest Rates

1. **Fixed-Rate Mortgages**: These mortgages lock in an interest rate that gets locked for the course of the loan. This predictability makes fixed-rate mortgages appealing to borrowers who seek stability in their monthly payments and long-term financial planning.
2. **Adjustable-Rate Mortgages (ARMs)**: Contrary to fixed-rate mortgages, adjustable-rate mortgages (ARMs) have interest rates that can varying during the course of the loan based on market interest rates. These loans may begin with lower interest rates than fixed-rate mortgages, making them enticing to borrowers hoping to sell or refinance before rates rise. However, the uncertainty surrounding future rate modifications implies that borrowers should be prepared to make possibly greater payments.

The mortgage's interest rate has a significant impact on the loan's total cost. Even little differences in interest rates can have a big influence on the overall amount of interest paid over the loan's lifetime. For example, on a $300,000 loan with a 30-year duration, a 0.5% variation in interest rate can result in almost $30,000 in increased interest charges.

Understanding how to calculate mortgage interest is essential for anybody interested in the real estate market, whether they are purchasing their first house, investing in property, or working in the sector. Mortgage interest can have a big impact on the total cost of a property over the course of the loan, so understanding how it is calculated and handled is critical.

The Basic Formula for Calculating Mortgage Interest

Mortgage interest is typically calculated using a simple interest formula. The annual interest rate is applied to the outstanding balance of the loan, divided by the number of payments per year. This formula can be expressed as:

Interest Payment = (Annual Interest Rate x Outstanding Loan Balance)/Number of Payments per Year

This calculation provides the amount of interest included in each monthly mortgage payment. Initially, when the outstanding debt is higher, the interest component of the payment will be greater. As the loan is paid down over time, the rate of interest reduces, and more of the payment is utilized to decrease the principal debt.

Example Calculation: How Interest is Applied to a Mortgage Payment

Let's consider a practical example to illustrate how mortgage interest is calculated and applied to a mortgage payment:

Suppose you have a 30-year fixed-rate mortgage for $200,000 with an annual interest rate of 4%. The mortgage is to be repaid in monthly installments, making the number of payments per year 12.

First, determine the monthly interest rate by dividing the annual interest rate by the number of payments per year:

Monthly Interest Rate = (4%)/(12) = 0.04/12 = 0.00333 or 0.333%

Next, calculate the monthly interest payment for the first payment, when the outstanding balance is still $200,000:

Interest Payment = 0.00333 x $200,000 = $666.67

This estimate shows that $666.67 of your first month's mortgage payment will go toward interest, while the remainder will be used to lower the principle. As the principal falls over time, so will the interest part of each payment, assuming the interest rate remains constant under a fixed-rate mortgage.

It's worth noting that most mortgages employ an amortization schedule, which specifies how payments are divided between interest and principal over the course of the loan. Interest is the primary component of mortgage payments in the early years. As the loan matures, the proportion changes, with more of each payment going to the principle. This approach assures that the loan is fully repaid by the conclusion of its term.

Factors Influencing Mortgage Interest Rates

Understanding the factors influencing mortgage interest rates is critical for navigating the real estate market effectively. These rates have a considerable impact on mortgage affordability and, as a result, potential homeowners' purchasing power. Several significant factors influence the interest rates lenders provide on mortgage loans.

1. **Economic Indicators and Market Conditions**: Mortgage interest rates are primarily influenced by the overall economic environment as well as individual market factors. Inflation rates, GDP growth, and employment statistics are examples of economic variables that influence lenders' interest rate decisions. For example, rising inflation frequently results in higher interest rates, as lenders must ensure that the real return on their loans remains positive. In moments of economic downturn, interest rates may be reduced to encourage borrowing and investment.

2. **Federal Reserve Policies**: In the United States, the Federal Reserve (often known as "the Fed") has a considerable influence in defining economic policy, particularly influencing interest rates. While the Fed does not set mortgage rates directly, its monetary policy decisions, such as determining the federal funds rate (the overnight interest rate at which banks lend to one another), have an indirect impact on the rates customers pay. When the Fed rises or reduces the federal funds rate, it affects interest rates throughout the economy, including mortgages, by changing lenders' costs of borrowing funds.

3. **Borrower's Credit Score and Financial History**: An individual borrower's credit score and financial history are two of the most important elements influencing the mortgage interest rate they can obtain. Creditors adopt credit scores to measure a borrower's creditworthiness, which are their chances of getting back the loan. Higher credit scores frequently end in lower interest rates since they provide less risk to the lender. Borrowers with poorer credit ratings or blemishes on their financial history, such as late payments or bankruptcies, may face higher interest rates or even be denied a loan.

4. **Loan-to-Value (LTV) Ratio**: The LTV ratio, which compares the mortgage loan amount to the value of the property, has an impact on interest rates. A lower LTV ratio suggests a higher down payment and less risk for the lender, which could lead to lower interest rates. Lenders face more risk when LTV ratios are high since it indicates that the borrower has less ownership in the property. To offset the lender's risk, higher interest rates may be required, as well as the purchase of private mortgage insurance (PMI).

Impact of Mortgage Interest on Monthly Payments

Understanding how mortgage interest affects monthly payments is critical for anyone getting into a mortgage agreement. The interest rate not only influences the overall loan cost, but it also determines the monthly payments that the borrower will make throughout the loan's term.

An alteration in interest rates can have an important effect on the monthly payment because interest is computed on the loan's outstanding balance. Fixed-rate mortgages have an interest rate that is set at the start of the loan period and does not change, resulting in regular monthly payments. However, the interest rate on adjustable-rate mortgages (ARMs) can change over time due to market conditions, resulting in monthly payment changes.

For example, a $300,000 loan with a 30-year term and a fixed interest rate of 4% will result in a monthly principal and interest payment of around $1,432. If the interest rate rises to 5%, the monthly payment will climb to around $1,610, increasing the borrower's financial burden.

Strategies for Minimizing Interest Payments

Borrowers can save a lot of money over the course of a mortgage by lowering their interest payments. There are many methods possible for accomplishing this purpose.

A mortgage's interest rate is determined by multiple variables, including down payment amount, the borrower's credit score and market conditions.

Borrowers can secure lower interest rates by:

- Improving their credit score through responsible credit use and timely payment of debts.
- Saving for a higher down payment might lower the loan-to-value ratio and qualify for lower rates.
- Comparing rates from several lenders to locate the best offer.

Another effective strategy for reducing the amount of interest paid over the life of the loan is to make extra payments toward the mortgage principal. This can be accomplished by:

- Making one extra mortgage payment each year, which can significantly reduce the loan term and the total interest paid.
- Adding an extra amount to each monthly payment, designated specifically for principal reduction.
- Making bi-weekly mortgage payments results in an additional complete payment every year.

Each of these strategies not only shortens the term of the loan but also reduces the total amount of interest paid, leading to substantial savings for the borrower.

Conclusion

The mechanics of mortgage interest and its impact on monthly payments are critical to the financial aspects of home ownership. Borrowers can better manage their mortgages by knowing how interest rates affect payments and implementing ways to reduce interest costs, saving money and potentially decreasing the life of their loans. Real estate professionals play an important role in teaching customers about these principles, ensuring that borrowers are well-informed and ready to make decisions that are in line with their financial objectives.

MORTGAGE APPROVAL PROCESS AND KEY CONCEPTS

The path to homeownership invariably leads through the critical phase of mortgage approval—a thorough process that compares an applicant's financial situation to the standards for loan issuance. This process not only assesses a potential homeowner's loan eligibility, but it also specifies the parameters under which financing will be granted, making a grasp of its complexities and accompanying financial measures critical for both borrowers and real estate agents.

The significance of this understanding extends beyond the mechanics of securing a loan; it includes a broader appreciation for how numerous financial indicators and market conditions interact to impact lending decisions. Mastery of this subject is not optional for real estate professionals; it is required to provide valuable advise to clients, ensuring they embark on their property purchasing journey with clarity and confidence.

The Mortgage Approval Process: Step by Step

1. **Initial Application**: The trip begins with the initial application, in which prospective borrowers provide lenders with detailed personal and financial information. This phase often include supplying paperwork on income, assets, outstanding debts, and personal identification. The richness and accuracy of this information are essential because it constitutes the foundation for each subsequent assessments.
2. **Prequalification and Pre-approval**: As previously discussed, prequalification and pre-approval are two distinct stages in the mortgage process. Prequalification is an informal assessment that offers purchasers an idea of how much they can afford with minimal documentation and verification. Pre-approval, on the other hand, is a more stringent process that includes a thorough examination of the borrower's financial history, with the result being a conditional commitment to lend a specified amount. This distinction is critical, as pre-approval provides a more solid foundation in property negotiations.
3. **Underwriting**: At this point, the lender's underwriting team undertakes a thorough evaluation of the borrower's

financial papers, credit history, and work status to determine the loan's risk. This procedure examines income stability and adequacy, financial behavior reliability, and long-term loan servicing feasibility. Underwriting is the backbone of the approval process, defining loan terms based on risk assessments.

4. **Appraisal**: Concurrently, an evaluation of the property in question confirms that its worth is appropriate for the loan amount. This assessment protects the institution from excessive lending and adds an extra degree of security to the transaction. An appraisal can impact the loan's terms, especially if the property's valuation does not match the predicted amount.

5. **Final Approval and Closing**: The final approval and closing step marks the end of the mortgage approval process. Here, the lender approves the loan after checking that all terms have been met and the property's valuation is satisfactory. This stage culminates in the signing of loan agreements, legal conveyance of the property, and the start of the borrower's repayment responsibilities.

Loan-to-Value Ratio (LTV)

The Loan-to-Worth Ratio (LTV) expresses a percentage comparison between the price of a mortgage loan and the estimated value of the property. It is determined by dividing the loan total by the estimated value or purchase price, whichever is lower, and multiplying by 100. For example, if a borrower applies for a $180,000 mortgage on a $200,000 home, the LTV ratio is 90% ($180,000 / $200,000 * 100).

LTV is an important indicator of loan risk from the lender's perspective. A lower LTV ratio shows that the borrower has an important ownership stake in the property, which decreases the lender's risk of loan failure. A greater LTV ratio, on the other hand, shows that the lender has a smaller ownership share and is taking on more risk. Lenders typically prefer an LTV ratio of 80% or lower; however, loans with greater LTV ratios may be granted with additional precautions such as Private Mortgage Insurance (PMI).

The LTV ratio has a direct impact on the loan approval procedure and the terms established by lenders. High LTV ratios may result in elevated interest rates or the necessity for PMI to protect the lender from a possible default. Additionally, debtors with high LTV ratios may face extra scrutiny during the underwriting process. A lower LTV ratio, on the other hand, may qualify borrowers for more advantageous loan terms, such as lower interest rates and PMI waivers, lowering the loan's overall cost.

Debt-to-Income Ratio (DTI)

The Debt-to-Income Ratio (DTI) reflects the capacity of a borrower to make monthly payments and payback loans. It is calculated by dividing the borrower's total monthly debt payments by their gross monthly income, shown as a percentage. This percentage includes all debt obligations, such as the next house payment, vehicle loans, credit card payments, and other debts. DTI is used by lenders to determine whether a borrower can easily afford the expected mortgage payment.

To calculate DTI, add all monthly loan payments and divide by the borrower's total monthly income. For instance, if overall monthly debt payments are $2,000 and gross monthly income is $6,000, the DTI ratio is approximately 33.3%. Lenders normally strive for a DTI ratio of 43% or below, however this varies depending on the loan type and lender requirements. Lower DTI ratios are preferred since they indicate that a borrower is financially stable enough to handle additional debt.

Improving one's DTI ratio might lead to increased eligibility for mortgage approval and better loan conditions. Strategies include paying off existing debt, particularly high-interest and revolving loans such as credit cards; raising income through additional work or finding higher-paid employment; and avoiding taking on new debt during the home-buying process. Reducing DTI not only helps to secure a mortgage, but it also promotes long-term financial health and stability.

Principal, Interest, Taxes, Insurance (PITI)

The concept of PITI is foundational in understanding the full scope of a homeowner's monthly mortgage obligations. It includes all of the parts that generally make up a mortgage payment: principal, taxes, interest and insurance.

- *Principal*: This is the portion of the monthly payment that goes directly toward reducing the outstanding balance of the mortgage loan.
- *Interest*: This component represents the cost paid to the lender for borrowing the principle.
- *Taxes*: Property taxes imposed by local governments are frequently included in monthly mortgage payments and stored in an escrow account until due.
- *Insurance*: This comprises homeowners' insurance, which covers damage and loss, as well as Private Mortgage

Insurance (PMI) if the down payment is less than 20%.

Lenders calculate PITI to determine whether a borrower can afford a mortgage. By calculating the total monthly PITI payment and comparing it to the borrower's gross monthly income, lenders can calculate the borrower's housing expenditure ratio, which is a significant consideration in loan qualification. In general, lenders prefer a housing expense ratio between 28 and 31% of a borrower's gross monthly income.

The full PITI evaluation assures lenders that borrowers can afford not just the loan but also the associated expenditures of property ownership. This assessment serves to reduce the risk of default by ensuring that borrowers have a realistic knowledge of their total financial commitment.

Private Mortgage Insurance (PMI)

PMI is a lender protection measure that applies when borrowers deposit an initial payment of fewer than twenty percent of the home's purchase price.

PMI protects the lender against borrower default by covering a portion of the lender's loss. This insurance is often required on conventional loans with higher LTV ratios, giving lenders an extra layer of security while allowing borrowers to buy a property with a lower down payment.

The cost of PMI varies with the down payment and loan amount, but it can significantly increase a borrower's monthly mortgage payment. PMI payments can range from 0.3% to 1.5% of the original loan amount each year, reducing overall affordability.

Borrowers may request PMI deletion after their mortgage balance reaches 80% of the home's original value. Furthermore, lenders are generally obligated to automatically eliminate PMI when the loan total reaches 78% of the home's initial value, as long as the borrower is in good standing.

Conclusion

The mortgage approval process, which focuses on important concepts such as LTV, DTI, PITI, and PMI, provides a complete framework for lenders to assess borrower eligibility and risk. These components, which are critical for comprehending the financial obligations of taking out a mortgage, emphasize the significance of comprehensive financial planning and knowledge for prospective homeowners. Real estate experts play an important role in assisting clients through these factors, ensuring they are well-informed and ready to make decisions that are in line with their financial objectives and capabilities. By grasping these concepts, professionals can improve their ability to negotiate the complexity of real estate financing, resulting in more successful and sustainable homeownership outcomes.

TYPES OF MORTGAGES AND FORECLOSURE MANAGEMENT

In our complete tour through real estate financing, we've previously covered fixed-rate mortgages, adjustable-rate mortgages (ARMs), and government-insured loans, each with their own set of characteristics and suitability for certain borrower profiles. These basic mortgage kinds are essential for both prospective homeowners and real estate experts to understand. However, to meet the different needs and financial capacities of real estate buyers, additional, specialized mortgage solutions are available. Jumbo loans and interest-only mortgages stand out because of their unique applications and restrictions. This chapter will go deeper into these two types of mortgages, providing additional insights beyond our previous discussions.

Jumbo Loans

Jumbo loans are an important financing option for buying high-value homes that surpass the conforming loan restrictions established by Freddie Mac and Fannie Mae. In areas with high real estate prices or for luxury properties, jumbo loans facilitate homeownership where standard loan limits fall short.

Characteristics and Requirements
- **Higher Loan Limits**: Jumbo loans surpass the federal loan limits, enabling the purchase of luxury properties or homes in significantly competitive markets.
- **Stricter Credit Requirements**: Due to the higher amounts loaned, lenders impose more stringent credit requirements, including higher credit scores (often above 700) and lower debt-to-income (DTI) ratios.
- **Larger Down Payments**: Borrowers typically need to make larger down payments, sometimes more than 20% to qualify for a jumbo loan. This rule reduces the lender's risk by guaranteeing that the borrower has adequate equity in the property from the start.
- **Proof of Financial Reserves**: Lenders may demand borrowers to demonstrate that they have adequate liquid assets or financial reserves to cover several months' worth of mortgage payments, increasing the likelihood of payback.

Jumbo loans play an important role in high-cost real estate markets, allowing wealthy purchasers to invest in premium properties. However, the bigger stakes require careful financial preparation and attention. Potential borrowers should consider their long-term financial health and the ramifications of taking on a substantial loan, especially in volatile market conditions.

Interest-Only Mortgages
Interest-only mortgages provide a unique payment structure in which borrowers pay just the loan's interest for a certain length of time. This arrangement can significantly lower monthly payments in the short term, offering flexibility for certain financial strategies.

Structure and Suitability
- *Initial Lower Payments*: By paying only the interest for the first 5 to 10 years, borrowers can reduce their initial monthly outlay, freeing up cash for other investments or expenditures.
- *Subsequent Payment Increase*: Once the interest-only period concludes, the borrower must start paying down the principal, often resulting in a substantial increase in monthly payments. This shift requires careful financial planning and awareness of future income stability.

Ideal Candidates
- *High-Income Earners with Irregular Bonuses*: Individuals who receive a significant portion of their income from bonuses or commissions may find interest-only mortgages appealing, as they can apply larger sums toward the principal during high-income periods.
- *Investors*: Some investors may prefer interest-only loans to maintain liquidity and allocate funds to higher-return investments, planning to sell the property or refinance before the interest-only period ends.

Interest-only mortgages carry inherent risks, particularly if property values decline or if the borrower's financial situation changes adversely. Borrowers must have a clear strategy for transitioning to higher payments or refinancing their loan to avoid financial strain.

Understanding Foreclosure
Understanding foreclosure is important in the domain of real estate financing because it is the legal procedure by which a lender tries to obtain the residual equity in a loan from a borrower who has ceased executing payments by imposing the sale of the asset used as security. Here, we look at the foreclosure process, management tactics, and the critical role that real estate professionals have in navigating these difficult circumstances.

Foreclosure occurs when a borrower ceases to pay their mortgage obligations, causing the lender to terminate the borrower's ownership of the property. The process helps the lender to collect the overdue loan amount by selling the home. Foreclosure has a substantial impact on the borrower's credit score and capacity to secure future financing, making it an important consideration in financial management and real estate.

The foreclosure process varies by state, although it often involves many essential stages:
1. **Default and Notice**: After repeated missing payments, the lender presents an advertisement of default to the borrower.

2. **Pre-Foreclosure**: During this period, the borrower can either pay the outstanding balance or sell the property through a short sale.
3. **Auction**: If the borrower cannot rectify the default, the lender may sell the property at a public auction.
4. **Post-Foreclosure**: If the property does not sell at auction, it becomes a bank-owned (REO) property, with the lender having the option of selling it through standard real estate channels.

The impact of foreclosure can be mitigated through proactive management and intervention strategies, both for homeowners at risk and for real estate professionals assisting clients.

Strategies for Preventing Foreclosure
- **Loan Modification**: Borrowers can negotiate with lenders to alter the terms of their mortgage, making payments more manageable.
- **Refinancing**: Replacing an old mortgage with a new one on alternative terms can bring financial assistance to distressed borrowers.
- **Government Assistance Programs**: Various programs offer support for homeowners facing foreclosure, providing alternatives to losing their homes.

Role of Real Estate Professionals
Real estate professionals are uniquely positioned to provide valuable assistance to clients facing foreclosure or looking to buy foreclosed properties:
- **Advising on Alternatives**: Professionals can guide homeowners through the options available to avoid foreclosure, such as loan modifications or government programs.
- **Navigating Distressed Sales**: For those unable to avoid foreclosure, real estate professionals can facilitate short sales or advise on the implications of foreclosure proceedings.
- **Investing in Foreclosures**: They can also assist investors interested in purchasing foreclosed properties, navigating auctions and bank-owned sales to find potential investments.

Foreclosure is an important part of real estate financing, demonstrating the serious implications of failing to satisfy mortgage commitments. Understanding the foreclosure process and various preventative options is critical for homeowners seeking to protect their financial future. Real estate professionals play an important role in assisting customers during these difficult times, whether by averting foreclosure, handling distressed sales, or investing in foreclosure properties. Their knowledge and assistance can make a significant difference in the result of foreclosure proceedings, highlighting the significance of professional counsel in navigating the complexity of real estate financing.

CREDIT LAW

Credit law is important in real estate financing because it provides a structured legal framework that ensures lending processes are fair, transparent, and accountable. This set of legislation is critical for protecting the interests of both lenders and borrowers, as well as ensuring a stable financial climate that promotes real estate market growth. Credit law includes a variety of legislation and regulations governing lending operations, credit reporting, and consumer protection in financial transactions. Its relevance in real estate financing cannot be understated, as these rules have a direct impact on how loans are constructed, applied for, and approved. Credit law protects borrowers from unfair lending practices and discrimination, ensuring equitable access to financial possibilities. These regulations establish explicit standards for lenders on responsible lending and risk management methods, which contribute to the financial system's integrity.

Key Legislation in Credit Law
- **The Truth in Lending Act (TILA)**: The Truth in Lending Act, passed in 1968, is a cornerstone of credit law, requiring lenders to disclose loan conditions and expenses to consumers in a straightforward and consistent manner. TILA applies to most types of credit, including mortgages, and ensures that borrowers are fully aware of their loan's interest rates, annual percentage rates (APR), repayment terms, and any associated charges. This

transparency allows consumers to effectively assess different loan offers, fostering competition and fair pricing in the lending industry.

- **The Fair Credit Reporting Act (FCRA)**: The Fair Credit Reporting Act, passed in 1970, governs the collection, transfer, and use of consumer credit data. The FCRA assures that credit reporting agencies and their information suppliers, such as banks and credit card businesses, deliver accurate and confidential credit information. It allows individuals to access their credit reports, correct inaccuracies, and be notified if information from their credit report has been used against them in a financial decision. This act is crucial to ensuring the accuracy and privacy of consumer credit data, which is used to make lending decisions.
- **The Equal Credit Opportunity Act (ECOA)**: The Equal Credit Opportunity Act prohibits discrimination in every aspect of a financial transaction regarding race, religion, color, national origin, marital status, gender, age, or because an applicant receives all or part of their income from a public assistance program. ECOA assures that all customers have an equal opportunity to acquire credit, and that lenders make decisions based on reliable and objective criteria. This legislation is critical for encouraging fairness and equality in access to financial resources, especially real estate loans.
- **The Real Estate Settlement Procedures Act (RESPA)**: The Real Estate Settlement Procedures Act compels lenders, mortgage brokers, and home loan servicers to provide borrowers with accurate and timely disclosures on the nature and expenses of the real estate settlement process. It also prohibits certain practices that could boost the cost of settlement services, including as bribes and referral fees. RESPA strives to protect consumers from abusive activities while also providing them with detailed information to help them make educated decisions about their real estate transactions.

Responsibilities of Lenders and Real Estate Professionals

Lenders and real estate professionals have a legal and ethical responsibility to comply with credit laws, ensuring fair practices in all aspects of real estate financing.

- **Adherence to Fair Lending Practices**: Lenders must ensure their lending practices do not discriminate against borrowers. This includes providing equal treatment in loan application assessments and offering reasonable accommodations for qualified borrowers.
- **Accurate Disclosure of Financing Terms**: Real estate professionals, including agents and brokers, must ensure clients understand the terms and implications of their mortgage agreements, including interest rates, repayment schedules, and any potential risks.

The compliance with credit laws significantly shapes the real estate financing landscape.

- **Loan Application and Approval Process**: Credit regulations ensure that the loan application and approval procedure is transparent and equitable, with all applicants being given equal consideration based on objective criteria.
- **Integrity and Fairness of the Real Estate Market**: Credit laws improve the overall integrity and fairness of the real estate market by enforcing standards for accuracy, privacy, and non-discrimination, hence increasing consumer trust and confidence in real estate transactions.

Credit law is the foundation of ethical and fair real estate finance, protecting consumer rights and defining defined roles for lenders and real estate professionals. Understanding these regulations is more than just legal compliance; it is also about creating a transparent, equitable, and trustworthy real estate market. As the industry evolves, being updated and adhering to these regulatory frameworks is critical for all parties in the real estate financing process, ensuring that the dream of homeownership is accessible and fair to all.

CHAPTER 6 - FOUNDATIONS OF REAL ESTATE AGENCY

DEFINITION OF AGENCY AND TYPES OF AGENTS

The concept of agency is central to the dynamic world of real estate, outlining the intricate interactions between agents and their customers, whether they are buyers, sellers, or both. Agency in real estate refers to the legal connection formed when an individual, known as the agent, is entrusted with acting on behalf of another party, the principle, in property transactions. This relationship is critical because it assigns agents considerable obligations and gives them the authority to make decisions that can have serious financial and legal consequences for their clients.

The value of agency relationships in real estate cannot be emphasized. These relationships influence the level of confidence and reliance that clients have in their representatives. A well-defined agency relationship guarantees that the client's interests are prioritized, directing the agent's actions throughout the buying or selling process. It provides an organized framework for conducting transactions while assuring clarity, efficiency, and legal compliance.

At its foundation, an agency relationship in real estate consists of a contractual agreement in which the agent undertakes to represent the interests of the client. This relationship gives the agent the ability to represent the client in talks and transactions involving the purchase or sale of property. The legal ramifications of this relationship are significant, as agents must comply to rigorous ethical and legal norms, including fiduciary duty.

Principles of Fiduciary Duty
The fiduciary duties that an agent owes to their principal are the bedrock of the agency relationship, encompassing:
- **Loyalty**: The agent must act solely in the best interests of the principal, avoiding conflicts of interest and ensuring that all actions and decisions benefit the client.
- **Confidentiality**: Agents are bound to keep the principal's information confidential, protecting their interests without disclosure to third parties unless authorized or legally required.
- **Obedience**: Agents must comply with the principal's lawful instructions, provided they align with the agreement and do not lead to unethical or illegal actions.
- **Accountability**: Agents are responsible for accounting for all monies and property associated with the agency relationship, ensuring transparency and integrity in financial transactions.
- **Disclosure**: Agents must fully inform the principal of all relevant information concerning the transaction, including material facts about the property and terms of the sale or purchase.

These fiduciary duties define the ethical and legal framework within which real estate brokers work, ensuring that the client's interests come first. Establishing an agency relationship is not to be done lightly, as it requires agents to fully commit to defending their clients' interests, with devotion and honesty guiding all decisions and actions. Clients must grasp the nature and ramifications of the agency relationship before picking an agent who will effectively represent their interests in the complex world of real estate transactions.

Types of Real Estate Agents
Real estate brokers play critical roles in navigating clients through the intricacies of purchasing, selling, and leasing property. Their responsibilities differ greatly depending on who they represent in the transaction. Understanding the various sorts of real estate agents and their separate responsibilities is critical for both practitioners and clients to guarantee that both parties' interests are effectively met.

1. Listing Agents (Seller's Agents)
Listing agents, or seller's agents, represent the seller in a real estate transaction. Their major role is to assist the seller in marketing and selling the property on the most favorable terms. Key duties include:
- *Property Valuation*: Advising the seller on the market value of the property and suggesting an appropriate listing price based on comparative market analysis.
- *Marketing*: Implementing strategies to market the property, including listing the property on various platforms, conducting open houses, and creating marketing materials.

- *Negotiation*: Representing the seller's interests during negotiations with potential buyers to secure the best sale terms and price.
- *Guidance and Compliance*: Ensure that the seller meets all applicable legal and regulatory obligations throughout the sale process.

2. Buyer's Agents

Buyer's agents act on behalf of the buyer, providing guidance and representation throughout the purchasing process. Their responsibilities include:

- *Property Search*: Assisting buyers in finding properties that meet their criteria, including location, size, price, and features.
- *Market Analysis*: Providing buyers with information on current market conditions and advising on fair offer prices.
- *Negotiation*: Negotiating with the seller or seller's agent to achieve the best possible purchase terms and price for the buyer.
- *Process Guidance*: Helping buyers navigate the complexities of the buying process, including financing, inspections, and closing procedures.

3. Dual Agents

Dual agency occurs when a single agent or firm handles each the buyer and the seller in the same deal. While legal in some states, dual agency requires clear consent from both parties and poses unique ethical considerations:

- *Conflict of Interest*: The dual agent must navigate a potential conflict of interest, balancing the fiduciary duties owed to both the seller and the buyer.
- *Full Disclosure*: The agent must fully disclose the dual agency arrangement to both parties, ensuring informed consent.
- *Impartiality*: The dual agent cannot advocate for one party to the detriment of the other, striving instead to facilitate a fair and mutually agreeable transaction.

4.Transaction Brokers (Non-Agency Relationship)

Transaction brokers provide facilitation services in a real estate transaction without entering into a fiduciary relationship with either party. They are not agents but serve to assist both the buyer and the seller in reaching an agreement:

- *Neutral Support*: Offering unbiased assistance to both parties in negotiating the terms of the transaction.
- *Documentation and Procedure*: Handling the necessary paperwork and guiding both parties through the procedural aspects of the transaction.
- *Limited Confidentiality*: While they must maintain a level of confidentiality, transaction brokers do not owe the same fiduciary duties as agents acting in a representative capacity.

Agency vs. Non-Agency Relationships

Understanding the distinction between agency and non-agency relationships is crucial in the realm of real estate. This differentiation not only affects the nature of the interaction between a real estate professional and their client but also the level of obligation and duty owed.

- **Agency Relationships**: In an agency relationship, the real estate agent owes the client fiduciary duties, including loyalty, confidentiality, obedience, and accountability. The agent represents the client, arguing for their best interests during the course of the deal.
- **Non-Agency (Transactional) Relationships**: Transaction brokers or facilitators assist in the real estate transaction without representing either party. They do not owe fiduciary duties but must treat both parties honestly, handle the transaction with professional competence, and provide factual information about the property.

The legal consequences of agency vs non-agency partnerships have a substantial impact on the actions and obligations of real estate agents. Agency relationships necessitate a higher level of care and impose particular legal obligations on agents, such as the duty to disclose relevant facts and conflicts of interest. Non-agency partnerships, while more limited in scope, necessitate transparency and fairness to ensure that no party is mislead.

Creation of Agency Relationships

The establishment of agency relationships in real estate is governed by both contractual agreements and state laws, underscoring the importance of explicit agreements and clear communication.

- **Written Agreements**: The most definite approach to establish an agency connection is to enter into a written agreement, such as a listing agreement for sellers or a buyer representation agreement. These documents clearly outline the scope of the agent's authority, duties, and the rights of the principal.
- **Verbal Agreements**: While verbal agreements can create an agency relationship, they are less advisable due to the difficulty of proving the terms and conditions of the agreement. Most states require real estate agency agreements to be in writing for enforcement purposes.

Agency relationships in real estate are also subject to state-specific laws and regulations that dictate how such relationships should be formed, disclosed, and managed. These laws might differ greatly, therefore real estate agents must be well-versed in the regulations regulating their respective regions.

PROFESSIONAL ETHICS AND LEGAL RESPONSIBILITY

Ethics in real estate encompasses the moral principles and values that guide the behavior of professionals within the industry. It's a foundational aspect that affects not only individual transactions but also the reputation and functioning of the real estate market as a whole. Ethical behavior in real estate transactions is paramount for several reasons:

1. **Building Trust**: Ethical practices build trust between real estate professionals and their clients, other professionals, and the public. Trust is crucial in real estate transactions, which often represent significant financial and emotional investments for clients.
2. **Credibility and Reputation**: Ethical behavior enhances the credibility of real estate professionals and, by extension, the industry. A reputation for integrity draws clients and develops positive working relationships among professionals.
3. **Long-term Success**: Ethical behavior helps real estate professionals achieve long-term success. Ethical businesses tend to thrive because they create loyal client bases and avoid legal troubles that can arise from unethical behavior.

Core Ethical Principles for Real Estate Professionals

1. Honesty and Integrity

Honesty and integrity are the foundations of ethical behavior in real estate. Professionals are expected to:

- Provide truthful information in all communications, including marketing materials, property descriptions, and disclosures.
- Avoid misleading or deceptive practices.
- Ensure fairness and transparency in dealings, giving all parties the information they need to make informed decisions.

2. Confidentiality

Real estate professionals often handle sensitive information related to their clients' personal and financial circumstances. It is their duty to:

- Protect client confidentiality at all times.
- Only reveal customer information with their full consent, unless legally required.

3. Fiduciary Duty

The fiduciary obligation requires real estate agents to give priority to the better interests of their customers over all else. This involves:

- Prioritizing the client's needs and objectives in the transaction.
- Disclosing potential conflicts of interest.
- Negotiating the best terms for clients and safeguarding their interests.

4. Professional Competence

Maintaining and improving professional competence is critical for offering excellent service. Real estate experts should:
- Keep up to date on industry trends and legal modifications.
- Seek ongoing education to enhance skills and knowledge.
- Accurately represent their level of competence and refrain from offering advice outside their area of expertise.

Legal Responsibilities of Real Estate Agents

Legal responsibilities are the foundation of a real estate agent's professional duty, ensuring that transactions not only meet ethical standards but also adhere to established legal frameworks. These responsibilities are crucial for protecting the interests of clients while preserving the integrity of the real estate sector.

Real estate brokers work in a complex legal environment that governs how transactions should be handled. Their legal requirements are varied, ranging from how they interact with clients and third parties to how they maintain and share information.

Real estate agents must navigate a myriad of state and federal laws that regulate the industry. This includes:
- **Real Estate License Laws**: Each state has specific regulations that govern the licensing, conduct, and continuing education of real estate agents. These rules ensure that agents have the expertise and ethical standards needed to effectively represent their clients.
- **Fair Housing Laws**: Federal rules, such as the Fair Housing Act, forbid discrimination in the purchase, sale, rental, or financing of housing regarding color, race, religion, national origin, familial status, gender or handicap. Agents must verify that all practices are compliant while promoting fairness and equality in housing possibilities.
- **Consumer Protection Laws**: These laws protect buyers, sellers, and renters from fraud, deceit, and unfair practices in the marketplace. Agents must ensure accurate representation of properties and disclose any known issues or defects.

Responsibilities Related to Disclosure Laws

Disclosure laws require real estate agents to inform both buyers and sellers of material facts that could influence their decisions about a property. This includes:
- **Condition of the Property**: Agents must report any known physical flaws or problems with the property that may impair its value or desirability.
- **Legal Encumbrances**: Agents are required to disclose any legal issues, such as zoning restrictions, liens, or easements, that could impact the use or ownership of the property.

Anti-Discrimination Statutes

Beyond the Fair Housing Act, agents must be mindful of state-level anti-discrimination statutes that may provide additional protections. Ensuring compliance involves:
- **Equal Treatment**: Agents must provide equal professional service to all clients and potential clients, regardless of protected characteristics.
- **Marketing Practices**: Marketing materials and methods should not convey any preferences, limitations, or discrimination.

Contract Obligations

In real estate transactions, agents are often responsible for drafting, reviewing, and ensuring the accuracy of contracts. This includes:
- **Purchase Agreements**: Verify that the conditions of the sale are clearly stated and agreed upon by each side.
- **Disclosure Statements**: Properly completing disclosure statements that accurately reflect the condition of the property and any material facts.
- **Compliance with Local Laws**: Ensure that contracts conform with local real estate rules and regulations.

Ethical Standards and Enforcement

In the real estate industry, ethical standards serve as a guiding light for professional conduct, ensuring that agents and brokers not only comply with legal requirements but also adhere to principles of fairness, honesty, and respect in their dealings. These standards are critical for maintaining trust between the public and real estate professionals.

Code of Ethics of the National Association of REALTORS® (NAR)

The NAR Code of Ethics is a landmark document in the real estate business, outlining the duties and ethical obligations of its members to the public, customers and other Realtors®. The Code of Ethics, which was established in 1913, emphasizes the significance of conducting business with integrity and upholding the greatest professional standards. It includes areas such as:

1. *Loyalty to clients*: Above all, prioritize the interests of the client.
2. *Avoidance of exaggeration and misrepresentation*: Ensuring all statements and representations are accurate.
3. *Cooperation with other brokers*: Promoting cooperation and fairness among all participants in the real estate transaction.

Compliance with the Code of Ethics is mandatory for NAR members, and the association has established mechanisms for enforcing these standards, including:

- **Ethics Complaints and Arbitration Requests**: Individuals, whether members or the public, can file complaints alleging violations of the Code of Ethics. These complaints are reviewed by local Realtor® associations, which can conduct hearings and determine appropriate disciplinary actions.
- **Disciplinary Actions**: Violating the Code of Ethics can result in fines, suspension, or even expulsion from the group.

Legal compliance is non-negotiable in real estate, where agents and brokers must traverse a complicated labyrinth of laws and regulations. Legal compliance guarantees that real estate transactions are done fairly, transparently, and equitably. It protects customers from fraud and deception, ensures fair housing possibilities, and upholds the integrity of the real estate market. Professionals must also follow legal regulations to avoid legal ramifications and maintain a respectable practice.

Impact of Non-Compliance

The repercussions of failing to comply with legal and regulatory requirements can be severe, including:

- **Legal and Financial Penalties**: Violations of real estate laws can result in hefty fines, legal sanctions, and compensation claims from harmed parties.
- **Loss of License**: Serious or frequent infractions can result in the suspension or revocation of a real estate license, thus eliminating the professional's ability to practice.
- **Damage to Reputation**: Noncompliance can harm the reputation of the individual agent or broker, as well as the entire sector, weakening public trust and confidence.

Conclusion

Ethics and legal compliance are fundamental cornerstones of the real estate profession, ensuring that agents and brokers conduct their business in a way that is not only legal but also morally correct and in the best interests of their clients. Maintaining these criteria is critical for promoting a fair, transparent, and trustworthy real estate market. Commitment to ethical behavior and legal compliance is more than just an issue of professional responsibility for real estate professionals; it is also a significant predictor of long-term performance and industry reputation. As the real estate sector evolves, all parties involved must maintain high ethical and legal standards.

AGENCY AGREEMENTS AND DISCLOSURE LAWS

Agency agreements in real estate are important documents that codify the relationship between a real estate professional (agent or broker) and their customer. These agreements serve as the foundation of the agency relationship, defining the scope of the agent's authority, the duties owed to their client, and the expectations of both parties involved in the transaction.

The major goal of agency agreements is to establish a clear understanding of the agent's role in the transaction, the services they will perform, and how they will be reimbursed for their efforts. Furthermore, these agreements provide legal requirements and protections for both the agent and the client, including as confidentiality, fiduciary duties, and the agent's promise to work in the client's best interests. Agency agreements provide clarity, which helps to prevent misunderstandings and disagreements, making real estate transactions go more smoothly.

Types of Agency Agreements

1. **Exclusive Right to Sell**: The exclusive right to sell agreement is one of the most prevalent types of listing contracts. Under this agreement, the seller grants a single agent or brokerage the sole license to promote and sell the property. The agent has the right to a fee regardless of who ultimately finds the buyer, ensuring that their marketing efforts are rewarded. This sort of arrangement encourages the agent to devote significant resources to selling the property, as their commission is assured if the property sells during the contract period.

2. **Exclusive Agency**: An exclusive agency agreement grants the seller the right to sell their home independently without paying a fee, as long as the transaction is not the product of the agent's efforts. The commission is payable if the buyer is found by the agent or another agent using a multiple listing service. This arrangement may appeal to sellers who want to maintain some flexibility in selling their property while still benefiting from the services of a real estate agent.

3. **Buyer Agency Agreements**: Buyer agency agreements define the legal relationship between a buyer and an agent, including the agent's responsibilities to discover homes that suit the buyer's criteria, negotiate favorable purchase terms, and guide the buyer through the purchasing process. These agreements ensure that the agent's loyalty is aligned with the client's interests, giving the buyer a devoted advocate throughout the property search and sale.

4. **Non-Exclusive Agreements**: Non-exclusive agreements, which are commonly utilized in buyer agency circumstances, allow the customer to use multiple agents. The customer is not obligated to purchase through any particular agent, and remuneration is often only paid to the agent who successfully locates the property the client decides to purchase. While this model allows the customer more freedom, it may result in less commitment from agents who risk not being reimbursed for their time and efforts.

Key Components of Agency Agreements

Understanding the core elements of agency agreements is essential for both real estate professionals and their clients. These components ensure that all parties have a clear understanding of the relationship's scope and terms, contributing to a transparent and successful transaction process.

1. Duration

The term of an agency agreement specifies how long the agreement is active and enforceable. It includes:

- **Start and End Dates**: Clearly defined commencement and expiration dates of the agency relationship.
- **Renewal Conditions**: Terms under which the agreement may be renewed, if applicable, including any requirements for notice from either party.
- **Termination Provisions**: The terms under which both parties may cancel the accord before its natural conclusion. This may include notice periods and any obligations or penalties incurred upon early termination.

Understanding the duration and associated conditions is crucial for planning and managing expectations throughout the transaction process.

2. Duties and Obligations

This section of the agency agreement outlines the specific responsibilities of both the agent and the client. Key points include:

- **Agent's Duties**: These may encompass marketing the property, conducting viewings, presenting offers, negotiating terms, and facilitating the closing process. Agents are also obligated to act in the client's best interest, maintain confidentiality, and provide accurate information.
- **Client's Obligations**: Clients may be required to provide necessary information about the property, ensure the property is accessible for viewings, and communicate openly with their agent. They must also refrain from entering into agreements with other agents that could conflict with the existing arrangement.

Clarity about duties and obligations helps prevent misunderstandings and ensures a cohesive working relationship.

3. Compensation

The pay clause specifies how and when the agent will receive payment for their work. Elements include:

- **Commission Rate**: The agent's pay will be either a percentage of the selling cost or a set fee. This rate is usually negotiated at the start of the agency relationship.
- **Payment Trigger**: Specifies the conditions under which the commission is earned and payable, often upon the successful closing of a sale or lease agreement.
- **Additional Expenses**: Outlines any additional expenditures that the client may be liable for, such as marketing expenses, and how they will be charged.

Understanding the compensation structure is critical for both parties. It ensures that the agent is adequately compensated for their services while also informing the client of any transaction fees.

Disclosure Laws in Real Estate

In real estate transactions, the idea of "caveat emptor" or "let the buyer beware" has been greatly modified by disclosure regulations that impose a legal requirement on sellers—and, by extension, their agents—to tell potential buyers of material facts about a property. These rules are crucial for ensuring the real estate market's fairness and openness, as well as protecting buyers from unforeseen complications and liabilities.

Disclosure regulations are anchored in the ethical and legal notion that buyers have the right to know about a property's condition and history before agreeing to a purchase. These rules ban sellers from hiding facts that could affect a property's worth or desirability, so that buyers can make informed judgments. For real estate brokers, adherence to disclosure regulations is a critical part of fiduciary obligation, strengthening their role as trustworthy advocates for their customers.

Types of Required Disclosures

Disclosure laws vary by jurisdiction but commonly include requirements to inform buyers about:

- **Property Defects**: Known physical defects, such as issues with the foundation, roofing, plumbing, or electrical systems, must be disclosed. This also covers any history of flooding or water damage.
- **Lead-Based Paint**: Because of the health dangers associated with lead-based paint, sellers of homes built before 1978 are required by federal law to report its existence.
- **Environmental Hazards**: Information about soil contamination, radon levels, or proximity to hazardous sites is often mandated for disclosure.
- **Zoning and Land Use**: Sellers must disclose any known restrictions on how the property can be used or developed.
- **Potential Conflicts of Interest**: Agents are required to disclose any personal interest they may have in the transaction, ensuring buyers and sellers are aware of any potential biases.

Failure to adhere to disclosure laws can have significant repercussions, including:

- **Legal Action**: Buyers may pursue legal action against sellers and their agents for non-disclosure, seeking compensation for undisclosed defects or issues that affect the property's value.
- **Financial Penalties**: Courts may impose fines and order the payment of damages to compensate the buyer for

the cost of repairs or remediation.
- **Damage to Professional Reputation**: Real estate professionals found in violation of disclosure laws risk damaging their reputation, losing the trust of clients and colleagues.

Best Practices for Compliance
- **Comprehensive Property Inspections**: Encourage sellers to conduct thorough inspections and share all findings with potential buyers.
- **Documentation**: Maintain detailed records of all disclosures made, including dates and the manner in which the information was provided.
- **Stay Informed**: Keep informed of modifications to local and federal disclosure rules to ensure compliance.

Effective disclosure policies do more than just meet legal requirements; they also defend the interests of all parties engaged in a transaction. Disclosures help purchasers understand what they're getting into and avoid pricey surprises. Transparency in disclosures can help sellers and their agents avoid future conflicts and legal issues, ensuring the transaction's integrity.

Disclosure regulations are a cornerstone of ethical and legal real estate business, ensuring that transactions are done transparently and fairly. By following these rules, real estate agents fulfill their commitment to defend their customers' interests, reinforcing the confidence that is vital to the agent-client relationship. Agents who navigate the complexity of disclosure not only meet legal responsibilities, but also contribute to a real estate market that values honesty, integrity, and informed decision-making.

DIFFERENT TYPE OF BUYERS

In the intricate world of real estate transactions, professionals often encounter individuals at various stages of the buying or selling process. These individuals can be classified into three distinct categories: clients, customers, and consumers. Understanding the nuances between these groups is paramount for real estate agents and brokers, as it dictates the level of service, loyalty, and duty owed to each.

The real estate industry's dynamics hinge significantly on the relationships established between real estate professionals and the individuals they serve. These relationships are governed by a mix of legal obligations and ethical standards, which vary depending on whether the individual is considered a client, a customer, or a consumer. The classification impacts how information is shared, the depth of advisory services provided, and the agent's fiduciary responsibilities.

- **Clients** are those who have entered into a formal agency agreement with a real estate professional. This contractual relationship affords the client the highest duty of care from the agent, encompassing loyalty, confidentiality, and diligent pursuit of the client's interests. Clients receive comprehensive services ranging from personalized property searches and market analysis to vigorous negotiation and transaction management on their behalf.
- **Customers**, in contrast, interact with real estate professionals without the binding commitments of an agency relationship. They might receive assistance from an agent, such as being shown properties or help with paperwork, but the agent's primary loyalty remains with the client they represent. Despite the lack of a formal agreement, customers are still owed honesty, fairness, and professionalism from the agent.
- **Consumers** represent a broader category, encompassing anyone potentially involved in a real estate transaction who has not yet established a working relationship with an agent, whether as a client or a customer. Interactions with consumers must be handled with care, ensuring clarity about the professional's role and obligations. Even preliminary conversations necessitate transparency to avoid misunderstandings about representation and advice.

For real estate professionals, recognizing and respecting the distinctions between clients, customers, and consumers is crucial for several reasons:
- **Compliance with Legal and Ethical Standards**: Proper classification ensures that agents fulfill their legal obligations and adhere to ethical guidelines, protecting the interests of all parties involved.

- **Clarity in Communication**: Clear understanding and communication of the nature of the relationship prevent conflicts of interest and ensure that individuals' expectations are appropriately managed.
- **Professionalism and Trust**: Agents who accurately navigate these distinctions demonstrate professionalism, earning trust from those they interact with, which is fundamental for building a successful real estate practice.

Professional interactions get more complex as the real estate sector advances. Real estate professionals must continually educate themselves on the legal and ethical implications of their interactions with clients, customers, and consumers, ensuring that they provide the right level of service and protection to each group. This commitment to understanding and respecting the differences among these groups not only safeguards the professional's reputation but also upholds the integrity of the real estate industry as a whole.

1. Clients in Real Estate Transactions

In the realm of real estate, a client is an individual who has entered into a formal agency agreement with a real estate professional. This agreement establishes a fiduciary connection between the agent and the client, with the agent legally obligated to serve in the client's best interests throughout the purchasing or selling transaction. The formation of this relationship is a deliberate act, usually solidified through a written contract that outlines the scope of the agent's authority, responsibilities, and the specific services to be provided.

Obligations Owed to Clients

Once the agency relationship is established, real estate professionals owe their clients a series of fiduciary duties, which are pivotal in ensuring the client's interests are protected and prioritized. These include:
- **Loyalty**: The agent must act solely in the client's best interest, avoiding any conflicts of interest and ensuring that all decisions and actions benefit the client.
- **Confidentiality**: Agents are obligated to keep the client's personal and financial information private and secure, sharing it only as necessary to execute the transaction and only with parties who have a legitimate need to know.
- **Obedience**: Within the bounds of the law, agents must follow the lawful instructions and preferences of their client, even if they might personally disagree with those choices.
- **Disclosure**: There is a duty to disclose all relevant information to the client, especially any facts that could influence their decisions regarding the transaction. This includes both positive attributes of a property and any potential drawbacks or defects.
- **Accountability**: Agents must account for all funds and assets related to the transaction, ensuring that the client's financial interests are meticulously safeguarded.

Services Provided

The scope of services an agent provides to their client is comprehensive, encompassing every stage of the real estate transaction process. These services aim to facilitate a smooth and successful transaction, aligning closely with the client's goals and preferences. Key services include:
- **Property Search and Market Analysis**: Agents assist clients in finding properties that meet their criteria, providing detailed market analyses to inform their decision-making.
- **Negotiation**: Agents use their market expertise and negotiation abilities to help clients get the best possible terms, whether they are buying or selling.
- **Contract Drafting and Review**: Agents ensure that all contractual documents accurately reflect the agreed-upon terms, protecting the client's interests and complying with legal standards.
- **Guidance Through the Buying or Selling Process**: From the initial search or listing to the final closing, agents guide their clients through each step, providing expert advice, coordinating with other professionals (e.g., inspectors, attorneys), and resolving any issues that arise.

2. Customers in Real Estate Transactions

In the intricate landscape of real estate transactions, the term customer represents a specific kind of relationship between an individual and a real estate professional. This relationship is distinct from the deeper, fiduciary bond formed with clients through an agency agreement.

Customers are individuals who engage the services of a real estate professional but without the formalization of an agency relationship. They may seek assistance from an agent for various aspects of the buying or selling process, but the agent does not represent them in the same way they would a client. The distinction lies in the level of obligation and loyalty the real estate professional owes to the customer versus a client.

Obligations Owed to Customers

While customers do not receive the same breadth of services or fiduciary duty owed to clients, real estate professionals still have significant obligations toward them, including:

- **Honesty and Fairness**: Agents must treat customers with honesty, providing accurate information about properties and transactions without misleading or withholding critical details.
- **Fair Dealing**: Even when there is no fiduciary duty, all transactions should be performed fairly to ensure consumers are not taken advantage of.
- **Disclosure**: While the duty to disclose is not as comprehensive as with clients, agents must still disclose material facts about a property that could affect a customer's decision.

Services Provided

Real estate professionals can offer a range of services to customers, which, while not as extensive as those provided to clients, are nonetheless valuable:

- **Access to Property Listings**: Customers can benefit from the agent's access to property listings, including those on the Multiple Listing Service (MLS), to find potential properties that meet their criteria.
- **Assistance with Paperwork**: The paperwork required in real estate transactions can be intimidating. Agents can assist customers in understanding and completing necessary documents.
- **Market Information**: Agents may provide customers with general market information, helping them make more informed decisions about buying or selling.
- **Property Showings**: Customers can often avail of property showings organized by the agent, giving them a closer look at potential properties of interest.

3. Consumers in the Real Estate Market

In the broader context of real estate, consumers encompass a wide category that includes individuals who are potential buyers or sellers in the market but have not formally engaged the services of a real estate professional through an agency agreement. This classification acknowledges that many people enter the real estate market with varying degrees of intention and commitment and at different stages of the decision-making process.

When dealing with consumers, real estate professionals are tasked with navigating initial inquiries and interactions with both care and professionalism. Key considerations include:

- **Clarification of Professional Role**: It's crucial for agents to clearly communicate their role and the nature of their professional relationships from the outset. This includes distinguishing between casual advice and formal representation.
- **Provision of General Information**: Agents can provide consumers with general information about the market, the buying or selling process, and what to expect when engaging in a real estate transaction without forming an agency relationship.
- **Respect for Consumer Privacy**: Until a formal relationship is established, agents must respect potential buyers' or sellers' privacy and confidentiality, cautiously handling any personal information shared during casual consultations.

Legal and Ethical Considerations

Navigating the initial stages of interaction with consumers requires a firm understanding of both legal obligations and ethical standards, ensuring that all parties are treated fairly and transparently.

Understanding Agency Disclosure

- **Timely and Clear Disclosure**: Real estate professionals must disclose the nature of their agency relationships with clients to consumers at the earliest practical opportunity. This clarity helps prevent misunderstandings about whom the agent represents and the scope of their obligations.

- **Informed Decision Making**: Proper agency disclosure ensures that consumers are fully informed before deciding to engage the services of a real estate professional, protecting their interests and promoting informed decision-making.

Respecting Buyer Rights
- **Fairness and Transparency**: All interactions with consumers, whether they become clients or not, should be marked by fairness and transparency. This builds trust in the real estate profession and protects the rights of all individuals exploring the market.
- **Equality of Service**: While the level of service provided to consumers may differ from that offered to formal clients, real estate professionals must ensure that every individual is treated with respect, provided accurate information, and not subjected to undue pressure or deceit.

CHAPTER 7 - CONTRACT MANAGEMENT

ELEMENTS AND TYPES OF CONTRACTS

Contracts, or written agreements, serve as the foundation for the exchange, lease, or modification of property ownership and rights in real estate transactions. Contracts play a critical role in these transactions because they not only specify the terms and circumstances of the transaction, but also offer a legal framework that protects the interests of all parties. Given the serious financial and legal ramifications, knowing the structure and enforceability of real estate contracts is critical.

A contract is a legally binding document created between two or more parties and enforced by law. To be recognized valid, a real estate contract must meet numerous legal conditions, including offer and acceptance, consideration, the capacity of the parties, the legality of the agreement's objective, and mutual consent.

Essential Elements of a Contract
- **Offer and Acceptance**: The process of making a contract begins with an offer, in which one party proposes the parameters of the agreement, followed by acceptance, in which the other party agrees to those terms. In real estate, an offer to purchase a property becomes binding when the seller accepts it, usually in writing. The precision of the offer and acceptance is critical, as any ambiguity might lead to contract-related problems.
- **Consideration**: Consideration is a thing of value that is transmitted by the parties as part of their agreement. The consideration in most real estate contracts is the acquisition cost established between the buyer and seller. However, consideration can also include other forms of value, such as a property transaction or a promise to execute specific tasks.
- **Capacity**: A contract is lawful only if the parties concerned have the legal competence to enter into it. This means they are legally capable of understanding and fulfilling the contract's terms. Most jurisdictions require that you be no less than 18 years old and of good mental health. Entities like corporations also have the capacity to enter contracts through their authorized representatives.
- **Legality**: The contract's objective must be legitimate and not violate public policy. A contract for a real estate transaction that involves the sale of a property for illegal activities, for example, would be void and unenforceable. Legality ensures that the contract's subject matter is within the bounds of the law.
- **Mutual Assent**: Mutual assent, or the "meeting of the minds," refers to the clear agreement between the parties on the terms of the contract. It signifies that all parties understand and agree to the contract's conditions without any reservations. This element is fundamental, as any misunderstanding or deception can invalidate the contract.

Types of Real Estate Contracts
Real estate transactions involve various types of contracts, each serving different purposes and containing unique terms and conditions. Understanding these contract types is crucial for navigating the real estate market effectively.
1. Purchase Agreements

A Purchase Agreement is a contract between a buyer and seller which describes the details and circumstances of a property sale. This comprehensive document includes:

- Property details (location, description)
- Sale price and payment terms
- Contingencies include finance approval and property inspections.
- Closing date and possession details
- Responsibilities of both parties (repairs, maintaining insurance)
- Signatures of both parties, making it legally binding

Purchase agreements are central to real estate transactions, providing a clear roadmap of the sale process and protecting both buyers and sellers.

2. Lease Agreements

Lease agreements describe the connection between landlords and tenants, outlining the conditions under which a tenant may occupy a property. Essential elements include:

- Rental period and renewal options
- Amount and payment arrangements for monthly rent.
- Responsible for security deposits and maintenance.
- Policies on pets, subleasing, and termination
- Rights and obligations of both tenant and landlord

Lease agreements ensure that both parties are aware of their rights and responsibilities, helping to prevent disputes during the rental period.

3. Listing Agreements

- Listing Agreements are contracts between sellers and real estate agents or brokers, authorizing them to market and sell a property on the seller's behalf. Types of listing agreements include:
- Exclusive Right to Sell: The agent has the exclusive authority to sell the property and obtains a fee independent of who discovers the buyer.
- Exclusive Agency: The seller may find a buyer on their own without paying a fee; however, if the agent gets a buyer, a commission is due.
- Open Listing: Multiple agents can market the property, but only the agent who brings the buyer earns a commission.

These agreements outline the agent's commission, marketing strategies, and the duration of the contract, aligning the interests of the seller and the agent.

4. Option Contracts

An Option Contract grants a potential buyer the opportunity to purchase or lease property at a predetermined price within a specified time frame, with no commitment to acquire. The customer provides an option tax, which is often nonrefundable. Option contracts are advantageous for buyers who require time to acquire financing or do due diligence but wish to lock in a purchase price.

5. Financing Contracts

Financing Contracts, including mortgage agreements and land contracts, outline the terms under which a buyer will finance the purchase of a property. Key components include:

- Loan amount and interest rate
- Repayment schedule and terms
- Consequences of default
- In the case of land contracts, the seller provides financing directly to the buyer, transferring the deed upon full

payment.

Financing contracts are critical for delineating the financial responsibilities and rights of the buyer and lender, ensuring clarity and legal recourse for both parties.

Understanding Contract Validity and Enforcement
For a real estate contract to serve its purpose effectively, it must not only be legally valid but also enforceable in a court of law. The validity of a contract hinges on its adherence to certain principles and the proper execution by all parties involved.

1. Legal Binding Nature of Contracts
A contract is legally binding when it contains all of the previously mentioned elements: offer and acceptance, consideration, capacity, legality, and mutual consent. Aside from these fundamental requirements, real estate contracts are frequently required to be in writing to be enforceable under the Statute of Frauds, a legal philosophy that requires certain agreements to be documented and signed.

2.Importance of Clear Terms and Proper Execution
The clarity of a contract's provisions is critical to its enforcement. Vague or unclear language can cause disagreements and misunderstandings, potentially declaring the agreement unenforceable or voidable. Proper execution entails not only signing the contract by both parties, but also ensuring that all legal procedures, such as notarization or witness signatures, are completed in accordance with jurisdictional laws.

3.Role of Contingencies
Real estate contracts contain contingencies, which are demands that must be accomplished before the deal is allowed to continue. Common circumstances include the following:
- Property inspection contingencies provide buyers with a set deadline to inspect the property.
- Financing contingencies require buyers to acquire financing by a specific deadline.
- Sale contingencies, dependent on the buyer selling their current home.

These contingencies safeguard the parties concerned by permitting them to opt out from the deal under specific conditions without penalty. However, they also introduce a layer of complexity to contract enforcement, as the failure to satisfy these conditions can void the agreement.

Conclusion
Real estate contracts are fundamental mechanisms that govern property transactions, outlining all parties' rights and obligations. These agreements must be properly structured to ensure legal validity and enforceability. The inclusion of explicit terms and adequate contingencies refines these contracts by customizing them to the parties' individual needs and concerns. The breadth and complexity of contract management in real estate highlight the significance of extensive understanding and meticulous attention to detail. Whether working with purchase agreements, leases, or financing arrangements, real estate professionals must navigate these legal waters with competence while maintaining the greatest levels of clarity, fairness, and professionalism.

NOTIFICATION AND ACCEPTANCE OF THE CONTRACT

In real estate transactions, the processes of notice and acceptance are critical in creating a legally enforceable contract. These stages guarantee that all parties involved have a clear knowledge and agreement on the transaction's parameters, transitioning from negotiation to formal commitment.

Notification serves as a conduit for communicating an offer or counteroffer, informing the receiver about the proposed terms. Acceptance, on the other hand, is the acknowledgment and assent to those terms, which essentially seals the deal. Both aspects are required; without proper communication, an offer cannot be accepted, and without acceptance, no legally binding agreement exists.

Notification in real estate transactions can take many forms, but its heart is the effective and clear communication of bids, counteroffers, and any changes to the terms of the contract. Traditional methods of communication include written notices sent by mail or courier. However, the rise of digital communication has resulted in a greater reliance on emails and online platforms for notification reasons.

Effective Notification Methods
- **Written Notices**: Traditionally favored for their formality and tangible record, written notices, whether mailed or hand-delivered, are a reliable method for notifying parties of contract terms or changes.
- **Electronic Communication**: Email and online platforms offer a quicker, more accessible way to notify parties involved in a real estate transaction. Many jurisdictions recognize electronic communication as a valid notification method, provided it complies with relevant laws and regulations.

The role of notification extends beyond merely informing about offers; it also encompasses any contractual changes, acceptance timelines, and conditions that must be met. Effective notification ensures that all parties have the necessary information to make informed decisions, fostering transparency and understanding in the transaction process.

Ensuring Understanding and Agreement
The clarity and timeliness of notifications are critical. Each party must be completely informed about the implications of the contract terms that are being published. This understanding is especially crucial in the real estate industry, where transactions frequently involve large financial commitments and legal obligations. Before proceeding to the acceptance stage, parties should be given the chance to evaluate, request clarification, and, if necessary, engage legal counsel.

Real estate professionals play an important role in this process, acting as middlemen to ensure that alerts are properly communicated and understood. They must ensure that all messages are precise, succinct, and include all relevant details to avoid misunderstandings and disagreements.

The procedure of notice and acceptance in real estate transactions lays the framework for a legally enforceable contract. It demonstrates the necessity of good communication and mutual understanding in developing effective and enforceable contracts. As we progress into the digital age, the methods of notification may change, but the fundamental concepts of clarity, comprehension, and consent remain constant.

Acceptance of the Contract
Acceptance in the realm of real estate contracts is a critical juncture where a potential transaction moves from negotiation to a binding agreement. For acceptance to be valid and result in a legally enforceable contract, certain conditions must be met.

1. **Constituents of Acceptance**: Acceptance occurs when the party receiving an offer agrees to the terms as offered, with no alterations. This agreement must be communicated back to the offeror in order to form a legal contract. Acceptance is frequently required in writing in real estate transactions, particularly those involving the sale of property, in order to comply with the Statute of Frauds.
2. **Time-Sensitive Nature of Acceptance**: Real estate offers often have an expiration date, making acceptance time-sensitive. If the offeree does not accept the offer within the stated timeframe, the offer expires and the offeree loses the option to engage into the contract on those terms. Delayed acceptance, therefore, can result in the nullification of the offer, necessitating a new discussion if the parties are still interested in moving further.

3. **Mirror Image Rule**: The "mirror image rule" stipulates that for an acceptance to be valid, it must exactly match the terms proposed in the offer without any deviations. If the offeree proposes any changes to the terms, this is considered a counteroffer rather than an acceptance, which the original offeror can then accept, reject, or counter.

Uniform Electronic Transactions Act (UETA)

The Uniform Electronic Transactions Act (UETA) represents a substantial shift in the way contracts, particularly those in real estate, are completed and approved. UETA, which was enacted to meet the rising reliance on electronic communication and transactions, legitimizes the use of electronic records and signatures by making them legally binding as their paper-based counterparts.

UETA enables for electronic notice of proposals and acceptance of contracts, increasing the ways in which parties can engage into agreements. This adaptability is especially useful in the fast-paced real estate industry, where being able to close agreements rapidly can provide a competitive advantage.

Under UETA, an electronic signature has the same legal standing as a handwritten signature, assuming that all parties to the transaction have agreed to conduct transactions electronically. This provision has greatly reduced the contracting procedure, allowing for faster and more efficient exchanges and approvals.

The use of electronic techniques for notice and acceptance has changed real estate transactions. Agents, buyers, and sellers can now use electronic papers and signatures to speed contract processes, from original offer to final acceptance. This efficiency not only speeds up operations, but it also improves accessibility by allowing parties to see and sign documents from almost anywhere.

The Uniform Electronic Transactions Act (UETA) has had a transformative impact on real estate transactions, fundamentally altering how contracts are executed and managed. Let's delve into the nuances of this impact.

Benefits of Electronic Transactions

- **Increased Efficiency and Accessibility**: Electronic transactions have expedited the contracting process, drastically reducing the time required to finalize agreements. The capacity to study, sign, and transfer papers electronically facilitates decision-making and can speed up the closing process. Furthermore, the convenience of internet transactions opens up real estate sales to parties who may not be in the same geographical location, extending the market for both buyers and sellers.
- **Legal Considerations and Compliance**: UETA establishes a legal framework that ensures electronic transactions have the same legality and enforceability as traditional paper-based transactions, as long as they follow the act's rules. This legal backing is critical for real estate agents who must handle a slew of regulatory regulations, ensuring that electronic contracts are both convenient and legally sound.

Challenges and Limitations

While UETA has facilitated significant advancements in real estate transactions, there are challenges and limitations to consider.

- **Security Concerns**: The transition to electronic transactions raises issues about data security and privacy. Real estate transactions contain sensitive financial information, making them a possible target for cyberattacks. Professionals must use strong security procedures to preserve this data and preserve client trust.
- **Digital Divide**: The transition to digital transactions requires access to and knowledge with technology. However, there is still a digital gap, with discrepancies in technological access and digital proficiency. This divide may erect barriers for some buyers, sellers, and even real estate professionals, thus limiting the reach of electronic transactions in the real estate industry.

Managing Offers and Negotiations with Electronic Transactions

The digital landscape offers real estate professionals new tools for managing offers and negotiations, but it also requires adaptability and careful consideration of legal and ethical standards.

- **Leveraging Technology**: Utilizing platforms that facilitate electronic signing and document management can improve efficiency and client satisfaction. However, professionals must choose reputable platforms that comply with UETA and offer robust security features.
- **Maintaining Legal Compliance and Integrity**: Ensuring that all electronic communications, offers, and acceptances comply with UETA and relevant real estate laws is paramount. This includes clear communication

about the nature of electronic transactions, obtaining consent for electronic dealings, and ensuring all parties understand their rights and obligations.

- **Addressing the Digital Divide**: Real estate professionals can play a key role in bridging the digital divide by providing resources and support to clients who may be less familiar with electronic transactions. This could include educational materials or alternatives for individuals who prefer traditional techniques.

Contract administration, particularly in the context of UETA and electronic transactions, is a significant component of modern real estate practice. The use of electronic technologies has resulted in indisputable gains in terms of efficiency and accessibility, completely changing the way real estate transactions is performed. However, this transition needs a rigorous examination of security, regulatory compliance, and the potential issues presented by the digital divide.

As real estate professionals negotiate this changing landscape, their ability to properly manage contracts—from initial offer and acceptance to term negotiation and dispute resolution—will remain a key indicator of professional competency and client service. Balancing the benefits of digital innovation with the timeless values of legal integrity and ethical behavior will keep the real estate business strong, vibrant, and inclusive.

MANAGING OFFERS AND NEGOTIATIONS

In real estate, the route from demonstrating interest in a property to closing a deal is facilitated by offers and discussions. This process is the foundation of contract formation, during which terms of sale are suggested, discussed, and agreed upon. Understanding this dynamic is critical for both buyers and sellers to successfully navigate the market and acquire transactions that fit their needs and expectations.

Offers and negotiations are the mechanisms for determining the price and terms under which a property will be purchased or sold. When an offer is accepted, it forms a legally enforceable contract. However, reaching that point frequently requires a series of conversations in which both sides change their demands in order to establish mutually acceptable ground. This step is essential because it shapes the financial and contractual landscape of the transaction, which influences both parties' satisfaction with the conclusion.

Achieving positive outcomes in real estate transactions entails more than simply making or accepting an offer. It necessitates intelligent bargaining and clear communication. Successful negotiators appreciate the value of rigorous preparation, clear objectives, and persuasive communication techniques when presenting their perspectives. These skills are crucial in negotiating the complexity of real estate transactions, allowing parties to establish agreements that are in line with their interests and aims.

Key Strategies for Effective Negotiations

- **Understanding Market Conditions**: Market conditions heavily influence negotiation techniques and offer strategies. In a seller's market, where demand exceeds supply, sellers can usually demand higher prices and better terms. In contrast, in a buyer's market, purchasers may have stronger bargaining power to negotiate cheaper pricing or specific contract terms. Real estate experts and their clients must assess current market trends in order to modify their negotiation methods efficiently.
- **Setting Clear Objectives**: It is critical to enter talks with specific, achievable objectives. Sellers may be required to set a minimum acceptable price or other sale conditions. Buyers, on the other hand, must know their maximum budget and vital specifications for the home. Having well-defined objectives allows parties to negotiate purposefully, making it easier to discover acceptable compromises and make educated decisions.
- **Effective Communication**: Real estate negotiations rely heavily on the capacity to express clearly and persuasively. This includes not just properly presenting one's own stance, but also carefully listening to the other side in order to grasp their wants and concerns. Effective communication can increase trust, promote understanding, and result in more productive conversations. Mirroring the other party's communication style, highlighting shared goals, and being upfront and honest about constraints can all help improve negotiating outcomes.

The Art of Handling Offers

Navigating through offers is a nuanced art that requires a deep understanding of the real estate market, keen negotiation skills, and an ethical approach to dealing with all parties involved.

The evaluation of offers is a critical step in the real estate negotiation process. Factors to consider include:

- **Price**: Is the proposed price consistent with the existing market value and the seller's demands?
- **Contingencies**: What conditions are attached to the offer? Home inspections, financing and the sale of the buyer's existing home are all common stipulations.
- **Buyer Qualifications**: Is the buyer pre-approved for a mortgage? Their financial readiness can significantly impact the transaction's smoothness.

Agents must analyze these factors critically, advising their clients on the merits and drawbacks of each offer, guiding them towards making informed decisions.

Counteroffers

Timing is critical in the counteroffer process. While prompt reactions can indicate excitement and keep the momentum continuing, it's also critical to pause and carefully consider the ramifications of the initial offer. This thorough thinking ensures that the counteroffer not only meets the seller's requirements but also appeals to the buyer.

For sellers, determining when to make a counteroffer—and when to accept an offer outright—requires a thorough understanding of the market, the property's distinguishing features, and the buyer's motivations. Buyers, on the other hand, must determine whether a counteroffer effectively resolves their issues or if additional negotiations are required.

- **Crafting Effective Counteroffers**: Effective counteroffers extend beyond basic price modifications. They cover a wide variety of phrases that can be adapted to the needs and priorities of both parties. For example, sellers may change inspection or financing contingencies to make the offer more appealing to the buyer, or they may negotiate the inclusion or exclusion of personal property, such as appliances and furnishings, which can have a considerable value and impact on the transaction. Real estate agents play an important role in structuring these counteroffers, bringing market information and negotiation skills to bear. They advise on which parts to change to improve the offer's appeal while protecting their client's interests.
- **Communication and Professionalism**: Clear, open communication is the foundation of effective counteroffer negotiations. It is critical to ensure that each party knows the rationale for the counteroffer and has the opportunity to respond meaningfully before reaching an agreement. Professionalism, defined as ethical behavior and courteous communication, is required throughout this procedure. Real estate agents must conduct these talks with integrity, treating all parties equally and maintaining a degree of decorum that encourages trust and respect. This strategy not only allows for smoother transactions, but it also protects the reputations of the professionals involved.

Managing Multiple Offers

The scenario of multiple offers presents both an opportunity and a challenge, requiring a strategic and principled approach to ensure a fair and effective resolution.

- **Transparent Process and Objective Criteria**: Transparency in handling various offers is essential. Real estate agents should develop and explain a clear, consistent method for analyzing and responding to offers. This procedure may include establishing deadlines for offer submissions and identifying the criteria that will drive decision-making. Using objective criteria to evaluate offers guarantees that the process is both fair and unbiased. The decision-making process takes into account factors such as the offer price, buyer financial qualifications, contingencies, and projected closing dates. By carefully analyzing these aspects, sellers and their brokers can choose the offer that best fits their needs while minimizing transactional risks.
- **Navigating Ethical Dilemmas**: Multiple offer situations can raise ethical dilemmas, especially regarding the equitable treatment of all potential buyers and the handling of confidential information. Real estate professionals must tread carefully, ensuring that their actions reflect the highest standards of fairness and discretion.
- **Effective Communication Strategies**: Keeping all parties informed is essential when managing various offers. Timely updates on the status of their offer, as well as comprehensive explanations for why it was or was not accepted, contribute to transparency and expectation management. Buyers can benefit greatly from constructive comments when an offer is not accepted, since it can help them modify their approach in future discussions.

Keeping all parties informed is essential when managing various offers. Timely updates on the status of their offer, as well as comprehensive explanations for why it was or was not accepted, contribute to transparency and expectation management. Buyers can benefit greatly from constructive comments when an offer is not accepted, since it can help them modify their approach in future discussions.

CONTRACTUAL CLAUSES AND DISPUTE RESOLUTION

Contractual clauses are the foundation of real estate transactions, describing the rights, obligations, and terms that govern the agreement between the parties. These clauses ensure that all participants have a mutual grasp of the deal's terms, decreasing the possibility of disagreements and misunderstandings.

Contractual clauses in real estate are meant to protect both parties' interests by creating a legal framework that encompasses all aspects of the transaction. These clauses lay the groundwork for the transaction, directing it from start to finish by establishing the buyer and seller's responsibilities and outlining methods for dealing with unforeseen situations.

Common Contractual Clauses in Real Estate
Several clauses are standard in real estate contracts, each serving a specific purpose:
- **Financing Contingency**: Ensures that the buyer can obtain finance for the acquisition. If the buyer is unable to acquire a financing, this condition allows them to terminate the contract without penalty.
- **Inspection Contingency**: Permits the buyer to have the property examined within a set timeframe. If substantial problems are discovered, the buyer may seek repairs, renegotiate the price, or withdraw from the transaction.
- **Sale of Existing Home Contingency**: For buyers who must sell their current house before purchasing a new one, this condition makes the new purchase contingent on the successful sale of their previous property.

These clauses protect the parties by outlining conditions that must be met for the transaction to proceed, offering a clear path forward or an exit strategy if those conditions are not satisfied.

Specialized Clauses for Specific Situations
Certain situations require specialized clauses to address unique aspects of a transaction:
- **Force Majeure**: This clause releases parties from their obligations if extraordinary events or circumstances beyond their control occur, such as natural disasters or political upheaval, preventing them from fulfilling their contractual duties.
- **Dispute Resolution**: Specifies the agreed-upon method for resolving disputes between parties. Options include mediation, arbitration, and litigation, each with its processes and outcomes.
- **Right of First Refusal**: Grants one party the right to match any offer the other party receives from a third party, ensuring the holder of this right has the opportunity to transact before anyone else.

Mechanisms for Dispute Resolution
Even with well-drafted contracts, disputes can arise. The mechanisms for dispute resolution are essential tools for addressing these conflicts without resorting to litigation.
- **Mediation**: A voluntary process in which a neutral third party assists negotiations between opposing parties in order to establish a mutually beneficial solution. It's non-binding, and either party can decide to pursue other resolution methods if mediation fails.
- **Arbitration**: An arbitrator or a panel hears both parties and then renders an outcome that is final. It's less formal than litigation and can be faster and less expensive.
- **Litigation**: The most formal dispute resolution method, involving a court case where a judge (and sometimes a jury) makes a binding decision based on the law. It can be time-consuming and costly.

Best Practices for Dispute Avoidance and Resolution

Dispute avoidance and resolution in real estate transactions are crucial for preserving professional relationships and ensuring a smooth process for all parties. Incorporating some best practices can considerably minimize the risk of disagreements and make their settlement easier when they do occur.

1. Clear Communication

Clear and transparent communication is paramount in preventing misunderstandings that often lead to disputes. All parties should ensure that:

- Terms and conditions are explicitly defined and understood by everyone involved.
- Changes to the contract are documented and reported to all parties quickly.
- Regular updates are provided throughout the transaction process to keep everyone informed.

Effective communication also involves actively listening to concerns and addressing them promptly, fostering an atmosphere of trust and cooperation.

2. Proactive Problem-Solving

Addressing potential issues before they escalate into full-blown disputes is a hallmark of effective transaction management. This involves:

- Identifying and discussing possible points of contention early in the negotiation process.
- Looking for mutually beneficial solutions to situations, rather than letting them fester.
- Utilizing negotiation tactics to achieve mutually beneficial outcomes.

Being proactive about problem-solving can save time, resources, and the stress of dealing with legal disputes down the line.

3. Legal Counsel

Learning when to seek legal advice is critical for understanding the complicated world of real estate deals and solving conflicts. Legal counsel should be sought:

- Before finalizing any contract, to ensure it is legally sound and protective of one's interests.
- Resolve disputes by analyzing legal issues and exploring potential solutions.
- To mediate negotiations that has stalled due to legal concerns or when a party is considering litigation.

Legal professionals can offer valuable insights and strategies for dispute resolution that respect both the letter and the spirit of the law.

Conclusion

Real estate contract management is a complex aspect of the property transaction process that necessitates a thorough understanding of contractual clauses, negotiation strategies, and dispute resolution processes. This chapter has covered the key components of handling bids and negotiations, the role of contractual clauses in determining transaction terms, and the many techniques for resolving disputes.

Real estate professionals can efficiently handle the intricacies of contract management by following best practices such as clear communication, proactive problem solving, and getting legal counsel as needed. These techniques not only help to avoid possible disagreements, but they also ensure that any difficulties that do emerge are resolved efficiently and fairly, preserving the transaction's integrity and the relationships involved.

CHAPTER 8 - SUPERVISION OF REAL ESTATE ASSETS

DISCLOSURE OBLIGATIONS AND PROPERTY CONDITION ASSESSMENT

In the complicated terrain of real estate transactions, the principle of disclosure is a foundation of legal and ethical behavior. Disclosure responsibilities compel sellers and their agents to tell prospective buyers of any known flaws or material information about the property that may influence the buyer's decision. This procedure is more than just a legal requirement; it exemplifies the dedication to transparency and honesty that underlies confidence between buyers, sellers, and real estate professionals.

Disclosure responsibilities cover a wide range of topics, from structural concerns and previous damages to legal encumbrances that may influence the property's usage or value. The goal is to offer buyers with a thorough understanding of the property they intend to purchase, allowing them to make educated decisions and avoid post-transaction issues.

Legal Framework for Disclosure Obligations

The legal requirements for real estate disclosure responsibilities are governed by a combination of federal, state, and local legislation, each of which adds levels of complexity to what must be reported throughout the transaction. At the federal level, disclosures may include the duty to tell buyers about the existence of lead-based paint in buildings built before 1978. State and municipal regulations may impose extra requirements, such as disclosures about natural risks, the history of land use, or even unique local environmental issues. These laws differ widely across jurisdictions, so real estate agents must be well-versed in the regulations that apply to their region of activity.

Real estate brokers play an important role in ensuring compliance with disclosure regulations. Their knowledge and counsel are critical in assisting sellers in determining what needs to be disclosed. Furthermore, they must comprehend the legal ramifications of omitting to report known flaws, which can include transaction cancelation, lawsuits, financial penalties, and reputational harm.

Agents must strike a balance between the seller's desire for a successful sale and their ethical and legal responsibilities to present buyers with accurate, complete information. This job includes advising clients on the scope of their disclosure requirements, as well as aiding with the production and presentation of disclosure documents.

Types of Required Disclosures

To ensure transparency in real estate transactions, numerous forms of disclosures have been standardized to inform potential buyers about a property's condition and history. These disclosures are more than just information; they are crucial for making educated purchasing decisions and protecting all parties involved legally.

- **Structural Defects**: Sellers must disclose any known structural defects in the property, such as problems with the foundation, roof, walls, or other vital components that may jeopardize the property's safety, use, or value. These defects could include large fractures, water damage, or any other problem that jeopardizes the structure's stability.
- **Presence of Hazardous Materials**: The disclosure of any hazardous items found on a property is critical for buyer awareness and safety. This includes the presence of asbestos, radon gas, or any other chemical that is known to cause health problems. Federal and state rules, such as the Residential Lead-Based Paint Hazard Reduction Act of 1992, specifically mandate the notification of these features.
- **Pest Infestations**: Sellers are required to report any existing or previous pest infestations, such as termites, rodents, or other vermin, that may impact the property's condition. Evidence of pest damage or treatments to address infestations must also be mentioned, as these can have a substantial influence on the property's appeal and value.
- **Previous Repairs and Ongoing Maintenance Issues**: Potential buyers must be made aware of any significant repairs or continuing maintenance difficulties. This includes details about substantial renovations, additions, or repairs performed to remedy flaws, as well as any known issues that have yet to be rectified. Transparency regarding these aspects assists buyers in determining future maintenance expenses and the overall worth of the property.
- **Zoning Restrictions**: Zoning restrictions can have a substantial impact on how a property is utilized and

developed. Sellers must disclose any existing zoning requirements or modifications that limit the property's use, such as prohibitions on building extensions, commercial use, or other major constraints.

- **Neighborhood Nuisances**: Disclosures may also include information on external variables, such as local nuisances or proposed developments, that may affect the property's desirability or value. This could include closeness to airports, landfills, or sources of noise or odor that could interfere with the quality of life on the site.

A detailed property condition assessment, usually performed by a professional home inspector, is an essential component of the disclosure process. This assessment gives an objective appraisal of the property's condition, highlighting any flaws that the seller or agent may not be aware of. The results of this assessment can help guarantee that all required disclosures are provided, lowering the risk of disputes and supporting a fair and transparent transaction.

Property Condition Assessment

A property condition assessment (PCA) is an important step in the real estate transaction process since it provides an in-depth analysis of the property's current situation. This inspection is often performed by a professional inspector who thoroughly examines the property to discover any problems, damages, or areas that require repair that are not immediately apparent.

Professional inspectors conduct PCAs in accordance with set rules, ensuring a thorough review of the property's structural integrity, systems (electrical, plumbing, HVAC), and external and interior conditions. They also inspect roofs, basements, and other potentially problematic locations. The findings are documented in a complete report that includes images, explanations, and suggestions for resolving identified issues.

Professional inspections are crucial for several reasons:

- **Identifying Hidden Issues**: Inspectors can uncover problems that sellers might not be aware of, such as hidden water damage, structural issues, or outdated electrical systems.
- **Informing Disclosure Documents**: The results of the PCA inform the seller's disclosure, ensuring that potential buyers are made aware of any known issues before finalizing the purchase.
- **Guiding Negotiations**: Information from the PCA can be a critical factor in negotiations, potentially affecting the sale price or terms of the contract if significant issues are uncovered.

Impact of Non-Disclosure on Transactions

Failing to disclose known defects or issues with a property can have significant ramifications on real estate transactions, affecting all parties involved.

- **Legal Disputes**: Non-disclosure of material facts can lead to legal disputes, with buyers potentially pursuing litigation against sellers or agents for failing to disclose known issues. These legal actions can be expensive, time-consuming, and detrimental to reputations.
- **Loss of Trust**: Transparency in disclosure is critical to establishing confidence between buyers and sellers. When sellers withhold information about property defects, it undermines this trust, potentially jeopardizing not only the current transaction but also the seller's or agent's future dealings.
- **Financial Repercussions**: For sellers, nondisclosure can result in financial losses, such as being required to pay for repairs post-sale or compensate the buyer for undisclosed issues. Buyers, on the other hand, might face unexpected repair costs, negatively impacting their financial investment and satisfaction with the purchase.

Best Practices for Fulfilling Disclosure Obligations

To successfully manage the complexity of disclosure in real estate transactions, sellers and real estate professionals must follow a set of best practices. These methods not only assure legal compliance, but also encourage fairness and transparency in the property sale process.

Developing detailed and comprehensive disclosure papers is critical. These paperwork should clearly detail any known faults with the property, no matter how trivial they appear. To achieve this:

- **Use Standard Disclosure Forms**: Many states provide standard disclosure forms that list common property issues to help sellers disclose known problems comprehensively.
- **Detail Repairs and Improvements**: Include a history of repairs, renovations, and improvements made to the property, specifying dates and the nature of the work completed.

- **Consult Professionals**: When in doubt about what to disclose, consulting with a professional inspector can provide clarity and ensure that all relevant issues are included.

The findings from professional property condition assessments (PCAs) offer invaluable insights into the property's state and should be integrated into the disclosure documents:
- **Attach the PCA Report**: Providing buyers with a copy of the PCA report offers a transparent, third-party assessment of the property's condition.
- **Highlight Significant Issues**: Clearly identify any significant issues uncovered during the PCA, along with any remedial action taken or recommended.

Ethical Disclosure Practices
Ethical considerations are paramount in the disclosure process. Sellers and their agents should strive to:
- **Err on the Side of Transparency**: When in dispute about whether to report a specific situation, choosing transparency is always the wisest option.
- **Avoid Misrepresentation**: Accurately describe the condition of the property and avoid minimizing or exaggerating issues to mislead potential buyers.
- **Maintain Open Communication**: Encourage potential buyers to ask questions about the property and provide honest, thorough answers.

The requirements to disclose and analyze property conditions are key components of real estate transactions, since they support the confidence and transparency required for successful sales. Sellers and real estate agents can ensure that transactions run smoothly by following best practice disclosure guidelines and implementing complete property assessments. Finally, a dedication to full transparency and ethical behavior not only protects sellers from potential legal ramifications, but also improves the integrity of the real estate market in general. As the industry evolves, these standards will remain critical in sustaining the concepts of fairness and trust that underpin real estate transactions.

LEGAL AND PRACTICAL ASPECTS OF LEASING AND PROPERTY MANAGEMENT

In the real estate industry, leasing and property management involve a wide range of actions and duties aimed at preserving and increasing the value of rental properties. Understanding the complexities of both the legal framework and actual operational components is critical for anyone working in this industry.
- **The Role of Property Managers**: Property managers act as intermediaries among owners of properties and tenants. Their principal responsibilities include promoting rental properties, screening possible tenants, negotiating lease terms, collecting rent, and managing the property's maintenance and upkeep. Good property management guarantees that properties are legally compliant, well-maintained and financially profitable.
- **Legal Foundations of Leasing**: The legal landscape surrounding leasing is multifaceted, involving various laws and regulations at the federal, state, and local levels. These rules control both landlords' and renters' rights and obligations, with the goal of ensuring that all parties concerned are treated fairly and equally.

Lease Agreements
Lease agreements are legally enforceable contracts that specify the terms and conditions under which a tenant may occupy a property. Essential components of a lease agreement include:
1. **Terms of the lease**: The duration of the lease period, typically ranging from month-to-month leases to multi-year agreements.
2. **Rent**: Rent amounts, payment schedules, and any rent increase circumstances.
3. **Security deposits**: Requirements for security deposits, including the amount, conditions for withholding, and return policies.
4. **Tenant and landlord obligations**: Repairs, maintenance and adherence to building laws and regulations are all

part of your responsibilities.

Understanding and properly crafting lease agreements is essential for avoiding disputes and ensuring the smooth functioning of rental properties.

Landlord-Tenant Laws

Landlord-tenant laws provide the legal framework that governs the relationship between property owners and their tenants. These laws address a wide range of issues, including:

- **Tenant rights**: Rights to privacy, secure and habitable housing circumstances, and defense against wrongful eviction.
- **Eviction procedures**: Legal processes that must be followed for evicting a tenant, typically involving notice requirements and court proceedings.
- **Property maintenance standards**: Obligations of landlords to maintain properties in a condition that meets health and safety standards.

Compliance with landlord-tenant laws is essential for property managers to avoid legal liabilities and foster positive relationships with tenants.

Fair Housing and Anti-discrimination Laws

The Fair Housing Act and other anti-discrimination laws are critical in the leasing and property management industries. These regulations prohibit discrimination on the basis of color, religion, race, gender, national origin, familial status, or disability at any stage of the lease process. To establish an inclusive and equitable leasing environment, property managers must ensure that all operations, including advertising and tenant screening, lease terms, and evictions, adhere to these regulations.

Practical Management Strategies

The day-to-day operations of leasing and property management require not just adherence to legal frameworks but also the implementation of practical strategies that ensure the smooth functioning of rental properties. These strategies encompass tenant selection, maintenance and repairs, and financial management.

1. Tenant Selection

One of the most significant elements of property management is picking good tenants. The tenant screening process aims to ensure that tenants will respect the property, fulfill their lease obligations, and pay their rent on time. Best practices include:

- **Credit Checks**: Assessing a prospective tenant's credit history to gauge their financial reliability.
- **Reference Verifications**: Contacting previous landlords and employers to confirm the tenant's reliability, promptness in rent payment, and overall conduct.
- **Adherence to Fair Housing Laws**: Ensure that the screening process is similar for all applicants and does not discriminate based on color, race, religion, gender, national origin, disability, or familial status.

2. Maintenance and Repairs

Effective maintenance and repair strategies are crucial for keeping properties in good condition and retaining tenant satisfaction. This involves:

- **Routine Inspections**: Periodic inspections can help discover and fix maintenance problems before they cause serious issues.
- **Prompt Repair Responses**: Addressing repair requests in a timely way are critical for tenant satisfaction and can keep small concerns from becoming costly.
- **Emergency Management**: Having a plan in place for emergency situations, such as natural disasters or major system failures, ensures quick action can be taken to protect the property and its occupants.

3. Financial Management

The financial stability of rental properties is critical to effective property management. Key aspects include:

- **Rent Collection**: Implementing efficient systems for collecting rent ensures steady cash flow.
- **Budgeting for Maintenance and Improvements**: Allocating funds for routine maintenance and property improvements helps maintain or increase property value.
- **Managing Operational Expenses**: Keeping track of and optimizing operational expenses, such as utilities, insurance, and property taxes, contributes to the overall profitability of the property.

Risk Management in Property Leasing

Effective risk management is critical for reducing the possible liabilities and issues of property leasing and management. Physical property damage, liability difficulties originating from accidents or injuries on the premises, and noncompliance with housing standards are all potential risks. Regular risk assessments can help detect possible areas of concern.

Strategies for mitigating risks include:

1. **Insurance**: Ensuring adequate insurance coverage for the property and liability can protect against significant financial losses.
2. **Safety Protocols**: Implementing and maintaining strict safety protocols and ensuring compliance with building codes enhance tenant safety and reduce liability risks.
3. **Regulatory Compliance**: Staying aware and complying with local housing regulations and building codes helps to avoid legal disputes and fines.

TYPES OF COMMERCIAL LEASING

Commercial leasing is an important transaction type in the real estate industry, affecting developers, investors, business owners, and a wide range of professions in between. Unlike residential leases, which are often standardized, commercial leases exist in a variety of formats and require a higher level of negotiation and modification to meet the specific demands of the business and the property involved.

Commercial leases are differentiated by their complexity, duration, and the considerable legal and financial considerations they need. They are not just meant to rent space, but also to align with tenants' strategic business objectives while protecting landlords' investment interests. Understanding the complexities of various commercial lease types is critical for both parties to negotiate terms that align with their long-term plans and financial objectives.

1. Gross Lease (Full Service Lease)

A gross lease, also known as a full-service lease, requires renters to pay a fixed rental sum while the owner covers all or most of the property's operational costs, including insurance, taxes and upkeep. This lease arrangement is especially frequent in office buildings and multi-tenant properties, where the landlord can effectively manage the building's overall expenses. Gross leases appeal to tenants who desire a fixed monthly payment due to their cost certainty. Yet, owners can impose a higher initial rent to account for fluctuations in operational expenses. Tenants in a gross lease arrangement benefit from the simplicity of a single, consistent payment, but they should be aware that this convenience frequently comes at a cost.

2. Net Lease

Net leases introduce a division of property expenses between the landlord and the tenant to varying degrees, classified into single net (N), double net (NN), and triple net (NNN) leases.

- **Single Net Lease (N)**: The tenant pays both the base rent and a part of the property's real estate taxes. The landlord pays for all other running expenses.
- **Double Net Lease (NN)**: Here, the tenant is responsible for the base rent, property taxes, and insurance premiums. The landlord typically handles maintenance and repairs.
- **Triple Net Lease (NNN)**: Considered one of the most landlord-favorable lease types, tenants pay the base rent, real estate taxes, insurance premiums, and maintenance costs. This sort of lease provides landlords with a more consistent income stream by shifting the majority of the property's operational expenses to the tenant.

Triple net leases are especially common in retail and industrial properties but require tenants to have a thorough understanding of potential operating costs. While NNN leases can offer lower base rent, tenants must budget carefully for the variable costs they will incur.

3. Modified Gross Lease

The modified gross lease is in the middle of the leasing spectrum, containing features of both gross and net leases. It provides a balance that may be particularly desirable in markets where tenants and landlords seek flexibility in expense allocation.

In a modified gross lease, the tenant agrees to pay a base rent, and the landlord and tenant agree on which running expenditures (taxes, insurance, and maintenance) the tenant will cover. This agreement allows both parties to customize the lease to meet their individual financial and operational requirements.

For example, a tenant may agree to pay the base rent plus utilities and janitorial services, while the landlord pays property taxes and insurance. The precise mix of expenses covered by each party can differ greatly, making each modified gross lease unique.

One of the primary benefits of a modified gross lease is the ability to provide the tenant with cost transparency and predictability while still covering considerable operating expenses for the landlord. However, due to the negotiated nature of these leases, both parties must be clear about whose expenses they are responsible for. Misunderstandings can result in disagreements or unforeseen charges later on.

4. Percentage Lease

Percentage leases are most frequent in the retail industry, especially in malls and shopping centers. This lease arrangement ties the landlord's revenue to the success of the tenant's business, resulting in a partnership-like dynamic in which both parties have a vested stake in the business's performance.

In a percentage lease, the tenant pays the base rent plus a percentage of any monthly sales that exceed a certain threshold. This arrangement encourages landlords to maintain their properties and assist their tenants in increasing their sales. A percentage lease, for example, may require a tenant to pay 7% of all monthly sales over $10,000 in addition to the regular rent. This agreement assures that the landlord benefits from high-traffic tenants, who add greater value to the property overall.

Key Elements and Negotiation

The key elements of negotiating a percentage lease are selecting the base rate, establishing the sales threshold, and agreeing on the percentage of sales to be paid in rent. These considerations must be carefully balanced to ensure that the lease is financially viable for the tenant while also providing attractive returns for the landlord.

Negotiating a percentage lease necessitates a thorough grasp of the tenant's business strategy and projections, as well as the market dynamics of the site. Landlords must consider tenant mix in multi-tenant properties, as one tenant's performance might generate traffic and sales for others, affecting overall property earnings.

5. Variable Lease

In the diverse world of commercial leasing, variable leases stand out for their adaptability to changing economic conditions. These leases allow for rent adjustments over time, ensuring that the terms remain fair and reflective of current market conditions or the financial performance of the tenant's business.

The core feature of a variable lease is its provision for rent adjustments, which can be tied to several factors:

- **Market Conditions**: Rent can be adjusted based on changes in the commercial real estate market, ensuring the lease remains competitive.
- **Inflation Rates**: Rent increases are tied to inflation rates, protecting the landlord's income from being eroded by rising costs.
- **Tenant's Revenue**: In some cases, similar to percentage leases, the rent might adjust based on the tenant's revenue, beneficial for businesses with fluctuating income.

Variable leases often include escalation clauses that clearly outline how and when rent adjustments will occur. These clauses specify the criteria for adjustments, providing predictability for both tenant and landlord. It's crucial for these clauses to be carefully negotiated and clearly articulated to avoid misunderstandings and ensure that adjustments are made fairly.

6. Ground Lease

Ground leases are a unique opportunity in commercial real estate because they allow tenants to lease ground for long periods of time—often several decades—while also developing or improving the property.

A ground lease divides ownership of the land from the buildings and improvements erected on it. This arrangement may appeal to tenants trying to develop a property without acquiring the land outright, as well as landlords looking to keep ownership while earning revenue.

The reversion provision in ground leases states that any modifications made to the land (buildings, structures) will revert to the landowner at the conclusion of the lease term. This structure compels tenants to carefully examine the long-term ramifications of their property investments, as they will not own the improvements indefinitely.

PROPERTY TRANSFER

Selling a property with an existing lease agreement brings a distinct set of issues and considerations. Unlike selling a vacant property, the existence of renters adds levels of legal and financial complication to the transaction. Understanding how to handle these obstacles is critical for landlords and property owners who want to complete a deal smoothly.

One of the key obstacles is balancing the interests of all parties involved: the seller wants a simple transaction, the buyer may have different intentions for the property, and the tenants' rights must be respected throughout the process. Furthermore, existing lease arrangements can have a substantial impact on the property's marketability and value, so sellers must understand and effectively communicate the details of these leases to potential buyers.

Understanding the legal structure governing the sale of leased property is critical. Both federal and state regulations safeguard tenants, preserving their right to occupy the property until the lease expires. Similarly, these regulations establish specific landlord obligations, particularly in terms of tenant notification and security deposit transfers. Understanding these legal criteria enables sellers to ensure compliance and prevent any legal problems.

Legal Considerations and Rights

The sale of a leased property doesn't nullify existing lease agreements, which remain in effect under the new ownership. This continuity implies that renters are often permitted to keep using the property under the conditions of their present lease.

Tenant Rights

Tenants' rights during the sale of a leased property include:

- Tenants have the right to stay in the property for the life of the lease, provided they follow the terms.
- Protection against eviction solely due to the property's sale, barring lease violations or terms that explicitly address changes in ownership.
- The expectation of timely and appropriate notification about the sale and any subsequent changes in management or ownership.

Landlord Obligations

Landlords have specific obligations to their tenants during the sale process, such as:

- *Notification*: Landlords must inform tenants about the sale and provide details about what to expect during the transition period.
- *Security Deposits*: The seller must transfer tenants' security deposits to the buyer, who then assumes responsibility for these funds.
- *Lease Agreements*: Sellers should provide buyers with copies of all existing lease agreements, ensuring the new owner understands the terms and obligations.

Impact on Lease Agreements

The sale of a leased property does not automatically change or terminate existing lease arrangements. Instead, these agreements are often transferred to the new owner while retaining the previously negotiated parameters. This continuity is critical for tenants, but it also has a big impact on the sale process and the property's appeal to potential buyers.

Lease termination upon sale is uncommon and typically needs specific stipulations within the lease agreement. More typically, leases remain identical, with the new property owner taking over the old landlord's contractual function. The transfer of tenants' security deposits from the sale to the buyer is an important part of this transition, as it ensures that the new landlord has these monies to cover potential damages or unpaid rent as agreed.

A property transaction can occasionally result in lease term renegotiation if all parties agree. However, tenants have the right to keep the original lease conditions unless they willingly consent to revisions.

Lease agreements may contain clauses that directly address the possibility of a property sale, such as:

- **"Sale and Leaseback" Agreements**: These arrangements involve the seller leasing back the property from the buyer post-sale, typically to continue operating a business on the premises.
- **"Assignment and Subletting" Clauses**: These clauses may allow the landlord to transfer the lease to a new owner (assignment) or let the new owner bring in additional or substitute tenants (subletting), subject to certain conditions.

Valuation Impact

Existing leases can both increase and decrease a property's value. Long-term leases with dependable tenants may boost attractiveness by assuring consistent income, whereas leases with below-market rates or short-term expirations may decrease attraction. Buyers must evaluate how the existing lease scenario fits with their investment objectives.

Due diligence is an important step for buyers, requiring a thorough analysis of all lease agreements to understand the financial and operational consequences of taking on the position of landlord. This procedure includes reviewing each lease's conditions, rental prices in comparison to the current market, tenant payment history, and any requirements for repairs or upkeep.

Buyers should also evaluate lease renewals, tenants' termination rights, and any existing disputes or compliance issues that may damage the property's value or the buyer's ability to operate it efficiently.

Process of Transferring Ownership

The process of transferring ownership of a leased property is a multifaceted endeavor that requires careful planning, clear communication, and adherence to legal protocols to ensure a smooth transition for the seller, buyer, and tenants.

1. **Listing and Marketing the Property**: The sale process begins with listing and marketing the property, highlighting its income-generating potential due to current leases. Sellers should prepare comprehensive information packages for potential buyers, including details about current leases, tenant histories, and the property's financial performance.
2. **Due Diligence and Closing the Sale**: Prospective buyers undertake due diligence, reviewing lease agreements, inspecting the property, and assessing its financials. Once satisfied, the parties move forward with closing the sale, which involves finalizing financial transactions, signing legal documents, and officially transferring ownership.
3. **Transferring Landlord Responsibilities**: The final step is the transfer of landlord responsibilities from the seller to the buyer. This includes:
   - *Security Deposits*: Ensuring that tenants' security deposits are accurately transferred to the new owner.
   - *Maintenance Records*: Providing the buyer with maintenance records, as well as any guarantees or service contracts.
   - *Tenant Communications*: Informing tenants about the change in ownership and introducing them to the new landlord or property management team.

Communication Strategy

Effective communication with tenants throughout the sale process is vital. Best practices include:

- **Timely Notification**: Informing tenants of the intention to sell and what to expect while the period of transition.
- Open Lines of Communication: Encouraging tenants to express concerns or ask questions about the sale and

addressing them promptly.

- **Reassurance**: Reassuring tenants that their lease agreements will be honored under the new ownership and that efforts will be made to ensure continuity in property management and maintenance.

Post-Sale Transition

After the sale, managing the transition of property management responsibilities is crucial for maintaining tenant satisfaction and property value. The new owner should:

- Review All Lease Agreements: Become familiar with the terms of all existing leases and tenant profiles.
- **Meet With Tenants**: If possible, meeting with tenants might assist to develop a positive relationship from the outset.
- **Ensure Continuity**: Work to ensure that property management practices remain consistent, or communicate any changes clearly and well in advance.

Conclusion

Selling a property with existing leases necessitates a comprehensive approach that respects tenants' rights and demands while satisfying the financial and operational objectives of both the seller and buyer. All parties can effectively traverse the complexity of such transactions if they follow a systematic procedure for transferring ownership, use effective communication tactics, and carefully manage the post-sale transition.

This chapter has discussed the essential concerns and stages involved in selling leased properties, with a focus on preparation, transparency, and tenant rights. As the real estate market evolves, understanding and efficiently managing the sale of leased properties is critical for real estate professionals, investors, and landlords seeking successful, mutually beneficial results.

EVICTION TYPES

Eviction is a legal procedure that permits an owner to expel a tenant from a rental property after an infraction of the lease contract or other significant problems. Eviction, a vital part of property management, is governed by specific laws that vary by jurisdiction but often include safeguards to promote justice and protect the rights of both landlords and tenants. Understanding the subtleties of eviction is critical for landlords to successfully navigate this difficult area of property management while maintaining legal compliance and cultivating a respectful landlord-tenant relationship.

Eviction allows landlords to resolve lease violations or inappropriate behavior, ensuring that the property is used responsibly and maintained correctly. It is a final resort, utilized when other methods of resolving the issue, such as communication and warnings, fail. Proper handling of evictions reflects on the landlord's management practices and can have an impact on the property's reputation and rental demand.

Legal Grounds for Eviction

Eviction laws are designed to balance protecting tenants from unjust removal with allowing landlords to regain possession of their property when lease terms are violated. Common legal grounds for eviction include:

1. **Non-payment of Rent**: The most common reason for eviction is the failure of the tenant to pay rent according to the terms of the lease. Landlords must typically provide a "Pay Rent or Quit" notice, giving the tenant a specific period to pay the overdue rent or vacate the property (3 days to as many as 30 days, depending on the state or local regulations).
2. **Violation of Lease Terms**: Tenants may be evicted for breaches of the lease other than non-payment of rent, such as keeping unauthorized pets, causing excessive noise, or subletting the property without permission. A "Cure or Quit" notice is usually required, offering the tenant a chance to correct the violation within a set timeframe (3 days to as many as 30 days, depending on the state or local regulations).
3. **Illegal Activities**: Illegal activity on the land, such as drug production or distribution, might result in prompt eviction proceedings. In these cases, landlords may issue an "Unconditional Quit" notice, requiring the tenant to

vacate without the opportunity to remedy the situation.

Types of Eviction Procedures

1. Pay Rent or Quit Notices: Pay Rent or Quit Notices are a landlord's first step in the eviction process for tenants who have not paid their rent on time. This notice serves as a formal demand for the overdue rent while also warning the tenant of potential eviction if the payment is not made within the stipulated period.

Issuing the Notice

The process for issuing a Pay Rent or Quit Notice is dictated by state law, which outlines:

- **Notice Period**: The specific timeframe given to tenants to pay the overdue rent, typically ranging from 3 to 30 days, but can vary widely by jurisdiction.
- **Documentation Requirements**: The notice must clearly state the amount of rent owed, the due date for payment to avoid eviction, and be delivered to the tenant in a manner prescribed by law, such as in person, by mail, or through posting on the property.

It's crucial for landlords to follow these legal requirements precisely to ensure the validity of the eviction process.

2. Cure or Quit Notices: Cure or Quit Notices are issued for violations of the lease agreement terms, other than non-payment of rent. These violations might include unauthorized pets, excessive noise, or failure to maintain the property in a clean and safe manner.

Process and Timeframe

The notice must specify:

- **The nature of the violation**: A detailed description of how the lease terms have been violated.
- **Cure period**: The period allowed for the tenant to rectify the violation, often ranging from 3 to 30 days depending on the jurisdiction and the nature of the violation.
- **Consequences of non-compliance**: A statement suggesting that failure to correct the offense within the specified time limit may result in eviction proceedings.

Landlords must ensure that the cure period provided is in line with state laws and that the notice is delivered following legal requirements.

3. Unconditional Quit Notices: Unconditional Quit Notices are the most severe form of eviction notice and are generally used in cases of serious lease violations. These notices demand that the tenant vacates the premises without offering an opportunity to pay overdue rent or correct a lease violation.

Grounds for Issuance

Common reasons for issuing an Unconditional Quit Notice include:

- **Repeated lease violations**: A history of the tenant consistently failing to adhere to lease terms despite prior warnings or notices.
- **Significant damage to property**: Causing substantial damage to the property's worth or safety.
- **Illegal activity**: Engaging in illicit operations on the property, such as drug production or distribution.

These notices typically provide a shorter timeframe for the tenant to vacate, often immediately or within a few days, depending on the jurisdiction and the severity of the violation.

Eviction Process and Tenant Rights

To navigate the eviction process, landlords must follow a defined legal procedure that ensures tenants' rights are respected and all acts are legitimate.

Once all preliminary notices have been duly served and the stipulated periods have expired without compliance from the tenant, landlords can move forward with filing an eviction with the court. This process typically involves:

1. **Filing a Complaint**: Landlords must file a formal eviction complaint in the appropriate court, outlining the

grounds for eviction and providing evidence of the lease violations or unpaid rent.

2. **Serving the Tenant**: The tenant must be officially served with the eviction lawsuit, often by a law enforcement officer or a court official, which includes details of the court date.

3. **Court Hearing**: Both landlords and tenants have the chance to present their cases to a judge. Landlords should bring all relevant documentation, including the lease agreement, any notices served to the tenant, and records of communication.

Tenant Rights and Defenses

During the eviction process, tenants retain certain rights designed to protect them from unjust eviction, including:

- **Right to Proper Notice**: Tenants must be given appropriate notice of eviction as defined by state laws before an eviction lawsuit can be filed.
- **Right to Contest the Eviction**: Tenants are entitled to appear in court to dispute the eviction, where they can submit facts and argue their case.
- **Legal Defenses**: Tenants may employ various legal defenses against eviction, such as proving the eviction notice was improperly served, demonstrating that the landlord has failed to maintain the property, or showing that the eviction is retaliatory in nature.

Handling Tenant Property Post-Eviction

Landlords must adhere to state laws when dealing with a tenant's property left behind post-eviction. This often involves:

- **Storing the Property**: In many jurisdictions, landlords are required to store the tenant's abandoned property for a specific period, allowing them to claim it (from a few days to several months, depending on the state or local laws governing the eviction process).
- **Disposal of Property**: If the tenant does not claim their property within the stipulated time, the landlord may be allowed to dispose of or sell the property

Impact of Eviction on Tenants and Landlords

- **For Tenants**: An eviction can severely impact a tenant's ability to rent in the future, damage their credit score, and cause significant personal and financial stress.
- **For Landlords**: While eviction can be a necessary step to protect their property and income, it can also be costly and time-consuming. The process involves court fees, potential property damage, and the loss of income during vacancy periods.

Eviction is a legal option given to landlords in the event of lease violations or unpaid rent, but it has considerable duties and risks. Throughout the process, both property owners and tenants must be informed of their relative rights and responsibilities. Landlords can successfully navigate the eviction process while minimizing the impact on all parties involved by following legal rules, honoring tenant rights, and carefully addressing post-eviction issues.

LEGISLATION ON FAIR HOUSING AND ETHICAL CONDUCT

The Fair Housing Act of 1968 was a watershed moment in the civil rights movement, notably addressing housing discrimination. It was passed in the aftermath of the civil rights movement, which saw tremendous struggle for equality in many facets of American society, including housing. This legislation was enacted to ensure that everyone has equal access to housing options, free of discrimination based on race, color, religion, gender, national origin, disability, or familial status.

The Fair Housing Act prohibits discrimination in nearly all housing transactions, including sales, rentals, and financing. It was a reaction to decades of institutional segregation and discriminatory policies that disenfranchised different communities and denied them the fundamental right to safe and affordable housing. The Act is significant because it promotes inclusion, diversity, and fairness in communities across the United States.

The passing of the Fair Housing Act was more than simply a legal milestone; it also signaled a societal movement toward recognizing housing as a fundamental right. Prior to its passage, discriminatory practices such as redlining and racial covenants were common, effectively banning minority communities from specific neighborhoods and denying them access to mortgage financing. The law has developed over time, with revisions strengthening its protections, such as the inclusion of disability and familial status on the list of protected classes in 1988.

Housing Transactions Covered

The Fair Housing Act encompasses a wide range of housing-related transactions. This includes:

- **Rentals**: Prohibiting discrimination in the leasing of apartments or homes.
- **Sales**: Ensuring equal opportunity in the purchase of residential property.
- **Financing**: Guarding against discrimination in mortgage lending, including terms and conditions, application processes, and foreclosures.
- **Advertising**: Banning discriminatory language and preferences in housing advertisements.

These provisions ensure that persons have equal access to housing, free of bias or prejudice, across the range of housing activities.

The Fair Housing Act, together with state and municipal laws, is a key component in achieving fair housing options for all. Its comprehensive coverage of housing transactions and protected classes reflects a commitment to eliminating housing discrimination and creating circumstances in which every individual has the freedom to choose where they live without prejudice.

State and Local Fair Housing Laws

Additionally to the federal Fair Housing Act, some states and municipalities are implementing their own equitable housing laws. These laws frequently go beyond and beyond federal rules, protecting new groups of people or providing more thorough remedies for discrimination.

State and local legislation may provide additional safeguards to classes not covered by the federal Fair Housing Act. Examples include safeguards for sexual orientation, gender identity, marital status, source of income, and age. These policies aim to guarantee that every member of the community have fair access to housing options by expanding their coverage to a larger demographic.

Intersecting with Federal Legislation

Fair housing laws at the state and local levels, together with federal legislation, form a comprehensive legal framework that addresses housing discrimination. In circumstances where state or municipal laws offer more protection than federal statutes, the more rigorous provisions usually take priority. This layered approach guarantees that people have several options for seeking redress in cases of discrimination.

Property managers and real estate professionals must comprehend the subtleties of both federal and local fair housing legislation. Compliance with these regulations demands not only adhering to the broad principles contained in the Fair Housing Act, but also understanding the specific safeguards and criteria imposed at the state and municipal levels.

Beyond the legal requirements required by fair housing laws, ethical real estate practice includes a dedication to fairness, integrity, and transparency in all transactions and relationships.

Ethical real estate practice entails more than just following the law; it necessitates a commitment to treating all people with dignity and respect, assuring honesty in advertising and representations, and protecting confidentiality and trust. Ethical behavior promotes healthy interactions among property managers, tenants, purchasers, and sellers, resulting in a more inclusive and equitable real estate market.

Many professional organizations, notably the National Association of REALTORS® (NAR), have created codes of conduct outlining their members' ethical obligations. These codes frequently go beyond legal standards, emphasizing the significance of ethical behavior in creating trust and confidence in the real estate industry. Adherence to these codes reflects a commitment to the greatest standards of professionalism and ethical activity.

Compliance and Enforcement

Complying with fair housing rules is a critical component of ethical property management. It necessitates a thorough understanding of the laws themselves, as well as the execution of practices and policies that adhere to the spirit and word of these regulations.

Compliance begins with ensuring that the tenant screening process is equitable and does not prejudice against any protected class. Property advertisements must also adhere to fair housing standards, avoiding language that could be perceived as discriminatory. Furthermore, property managers must make appropriate modifications for renters with disabilities, ensuring that they have equal access to homes.

Fair housing regulations are enforced by a number of state, federal and municipal agencies. The Department of Housing and Urban Development (HUD) is a key federal agency that investigates complaints, conducts compliance assessments, and takes enforcement action when warranted. Penalties for infractions can be severe, including penalties, restitution to victims, and injunctions prohibiting future discrimination. Furthermore, property managers and landlords may incur reputational damage, stressing the need of following these laws.

Practical Implications for Property Management

Fair housing principles must be included into property management not only legally, but also morally and ethically. It guarantees that every person has equal access to housing and is treated with dignity and respect throughout their tenancy. Regular staff training on fair housing laws and ethical practices, developing and implementing non-discriminatory policies for tenant screening and selection, and ensuring that all marketing materials are inclusive and welcoming to all individuals are examples of strategies for integrating these principles.

Conclusion

Legislation governing fair housing and ethical behavior is the foundation of a just and equitable housing market. Understanding and implementing these regulations is important for property managers and real estate agents because it fosters communities in which everyone has the chance to find a home without fear of discrimination. The real estate business may uphold the greatest standards of equity and respect by diligently adhering to fair housing principles, ongoing education, and ethical property management methods, thereby positively contributing to the social fabric of communities around the country.

CHAPTER 9 – TITLE TRANSITION

DIFFERENCE BETWEEN TITLE AND DEEDS

Legislation governing fair housing and ethical behavior is the foundation of a just and equitable housing market. Understanding and implementing these regulations is important for property managers and real estate agents because it fosters communities in which everyone has the chance to find a home without fear of discrimination. The real estate business may uphold the greatest standards of equity and respect by diligently adhering to fair housing principles, ongoing education, and ethical property management methods, thereby positively contributing to the social fabric of communities around the country.

- **Title**: The title represents the legal right to use, own and dispose of property. It is not a literal document, but rather a notion that represents ownership and the "bundle of rights" that come with owning actual property. These rights may include possession, control, exclusion, enjoyment, and disposition. Title refers to the cumulative legal rights to a property. When you have title to a piece of real land, you have the legal right to claim ownership. This notion is crucial in the real estate sector since it supports every transaction and ensures that the individual selling the property has the legal right to do so.
- **Deeds**: On the contrary, a deed is a physical document that permits the seller to transfer property title to the buyer. It is tangible proof of the transfer, containing detailed information about the property, the persons involved, and the terms of the agreement. Deeds play an important role in real estate transactions by establishing a legal foundation for transferring ownership. They must be carefully designed, which frequently necessitates legal knowledge to assure correctness and conformity with state regulations. Once executed, a deed needs to be submitted with the local government, usually in the county where the property is situated, in order for the transfer to become public record and maintain the new owner's rights.

Title vs. Deeds: Key Differences

The major distinction between title and deeds is their nature and function in real estate transactions. The title is a wide notion that incorporates the legal rights that come with property ownership. It is not represented by a tangible document, but rather by the owner's legal claim to the property, which includes the right to use, lease, sell, or transfer it in other ways. Deeds, on the other hand, are physical legal documents that enable the transfer of ownership from one party to another. They serve as an official record of the transaction, documenting the circumstances of the property transfer, such as the parties involved, the property description, and the terms under which the property is transferred.

The execution and delivery of a deed establishes a transfer of title. A property transaction can be regarded genuine and legal if the deed is correctly drafted, signed, and, most crucially, registered in public records. This recording acts as official notice of the transfer of property ownership and is critical for maintaining the new owner's rights to the property.

The Role of Deeds in Establishing Title

The conveyance of real estate from one person to another is legally established by the deed. This document is required not only to document the transaction, but also to outline the conditions under which the title is transferred. Various types of deeds, such as warranty and quitclaim deeds, provide varying degrees of protection and title guarantee.

- **Warranty Deeds**: Provide the buyer with the maximum level of protection possible, ensuring that the seller has clear title to the property and the right to sell it. They also protect against any future claims against the title.
- **Quitclaim Deeds**: Provide no warranties about the title's quality. They are often used between family members or to clear up title issues, transferring whatever interest the grantor has in the property, if any.

The choice of deed has significant implications for both the buyer and seller, affecting the security of the transaction and the future rights of the property owner.

STATUS OF THE TITLE

Understanding a property's title status is a critical step in the real estate purchase process. The title to a property is a legal notion that represents ownership rights, such as the right to hold, use, and transfer it. The status of a title can have a substantial impact on the practicality and security of real estate transactions, affecting all parties involved, including sellers, buyers, and financial institutions.

The condition of a property's title affects whether ownership can be transferred without claims, liens, or other legal encumbrances that could impair the buyer's rights. A clear and unambiguous title is necessary for the legal transfer of property ownership and obtaining mortgage financing, as lenders often require a clean title to protect their investment.

1. Clear Title: A clear title is one that contains no legal concerns or conflicts about the property's ownership. It indicates that the property owner has an indisputable right to sell or transfer the property and that the buyer can safely assume ownership without concerns of third-party claims. Significance in Real Estate:

- **Facilitates Transactions**: A clear title enables smooth property transactions, as there are no disputes or encumbrances to resolve before the sale.
- **Attracts Buyers**: Properties with a clear title are more attractive to buyers and investors, as they provide security and peace of mind regarding ownership rights.

2. Cloudy (or Clouded) Title: A cloudy title, also known as a clouded title, refers to any irregularity or issue in the documentation or historical chain of title that raises questions about the true ownership of the property. This can involve unsettled liens, boundary conflicts, and inaccuracies in public documents. Challenges Presented:

- **Impedes Transactions**: A clouded title can significantly delay or derail real estate transactions until the issues are resolved.
- **Legal and Financial Risks**: Both sellers and buyers face risks with a cloudy title. Sellers may find it difficult to sell the property, and buyers may inherit the unresolved issues, affecting their ownership rights.

Resolving issues that cloud a title often involves legal actions, such as filing a quiet title lawsuit to establish clear ownership, or utilizing title insurance to protect against claims. Conducting a comprehensive title search and examination is crucial for identifying any potential issues early in the transaction process.

- **Quiet Title Actions**: A legal procedure for resolving disputes or claims against a property's title, thereby clarifying and establishing the owner's rights.
- **Title Insurance**: Buyers and lenders are financially protected from losses caused by title flaws, including those that were not detected during the original investigation.

Clear vs. Cloudy Title: Implications for Transactions

The distinction between clear and cloudy titles is not just a matter of legal technicality; it profoundly influences the dynamics of real estate transactions. This part of the chapter delves into how each type of title status impacts both sellers and buyers, highlighting the crucial steps necessary to navigate potential challenges.

For Sellers

- **Clear Title**: Sellers with clear title can approach the market with confidence, knowing that their property is free of any encumbrances that could jeopardize the sale. A clear title speeds up the transaction process, attracts a larger pool of possible purchasers, and may command a higher selling price due to the buyer's reduced risk.
- **Cloudy Title**: Sellers with a clouded title must address and rectify any difficulties before proceeding with the transaction. This could include legal actions like filing for a quiet title or resolving outstanding liens or disputes. The procedure can be time-consuming and costly, potentially affecting the property's marketability and sale price. Sellers must be proactive in resolving title difficulties to avoid transaction delays and loss of buyer interest.

For Buyers

- **Clear Title**: Buyers are generally more inclined to pursue properties with a clear title, ensuring a smoother transition of ownership and peace of mind regarding their investment. Prior to purchase, buyers should conduct thorough due diligence, including a comprehensive title search and review, to confirm the status of the title.
- **Cloudy Title**: When considering a property with a cloudy title, buyers must weigh the risks and potential for future disputes. Due diligence is critical, and it is often necessary to seek legal guidance to properly grasp the implications. Title insurance becomes an essential consideration for buyers in these scenarios, offering protection against unforeseen claims and liabilities.

The Critical Role of Due Diligence

Due diligence is crucial in determining title status and assuring a property's legal transfer. This includes doing a thorough title search to identify any concerns that may impair the title's clarity, such as unpaid taxes, liens, or inaccuracies in public records. Buyers and sellers both benefit from this procedure, which seeks to identify and handle possible issues before they affect the deal.

Legal and professional assistance is frequently required to overcome the intricacies of title transfer. This procedure is primarily reliant on real estate professionals, like attorneys, agents and title companies. They ensure that all components of the title are thoroughly reviewed and any concerns are rectified, allowing for a lawful and secure transfer of property ownership.

The state of a property's title, whether clear or hazy, has important ramifications for real estate transactions, influencing everything from the sale process to the security of ownership after the purchase. Anyone dealing in real estate must understand the differences between these statuses, as well as the need of due diligence and legal resolution options. Finally, preserving a clear title not only protects the interests of buyers and sellers, but it also maintains the integrity of the real estate market in general.

TITLE PREREQUISITES

In the realm of real estate transactions, verifying that a title fits specific requirements is critical to a seamless and legal transfer of property. A title represents legal ownership and the ability to use the property, therefore its validation is critical for both purchasers and sellers. The requirements for a valid title include a number of legal standards and checks aimed to ensure the title's legality and the seller's authority to transfer ownership without legal restrictions.

Meeting title prerequisites is critical for sellers since it demonstrates their legal right to sell the property and ensures that the transaction goes smoothly. Verifying these conditions safeguards buyers from future claims or disputes over property title, giving them piece of mind and confidence in their investment.

Understanding Marketable Title

A marketable title is one that is free from serious legal questions or disputes, ensuring that a buyer takes ownership without facing potential litigation or claims from third parties. It is a key concept in real estate that influences the transaction's viability and the property's desirability.

A marketable title often satisfies the following criteria:

- **Clear History of Ownership**: The title should have a well-documented history of ownership transfers, free from gaps or ambiguities that could question the current seller's ownership rights.
- **No Significant Liens or Encumbrances**: Liens, such as those placed by creditors, or encumbrances, like easements, can limit the owner's rights to the property. A marketable title should be free from any liens or encumbrances that could adversely affect the buyer's use and enjoyment of the property.
- **Absence of Pending Legal Disputes**: The title should not be the subject of ongoing legal disputes regarding property boundaries, ownership claims, or other issues that could jeopardize the buyer's rightful ownership.

Marketability is crucial because it directly impacts the buyer's ability to use the property freely and to sell it in the future. Buyers typically require a marketable title before proceeding with a purchase, and lenders often require it before approving a mortgage, making it a fundamental aspect of real estate transactions.

- **Challenges to Marketable Title**: Marketability of a title can be compromised by several factors, each posing unique challenges to the conveyance process. Addressing these problems is critical to achieving a successful transaction and respecting the interests of all parties concerned.
- **Unresolved Claims**: Unresolved claims against a property, such as those from heirs or previous owners, can significantly impact a title's marketability. These claims may arise from disputes over wills, divorce settlements, or alleged errors in past sales. Resolving such claims often requires legal action, such as quiet title lawsuits, to affirm the seller's rightful ownership.
- **Boundary Disputes**: Discrepancies in property boundaries can also cloud a title's marketability. Such disputes may stem from inaccurate or outdated property descriptions in deeds, conflicting surveys, or encroachments by neighboring properties. Resolving boundary disputes may involve renegotiating property lines, purchasing additional land, or obtaining easements.
- **Errors in Public Records**: Mistakes in public records, like property descriptions, incorrect names or clerical errors, can harm a title's marketability. To fix these errors, identify the inaccuracies, collect supporting documents, and file corrections with the appropriate public office. This process, while possibly time-consuming, is crucial to clearing the title.

Understanding Insurable Title

An insurable title, like a marketable title, emphasizes the title's insurability rather than its defect-free status. It recognizes that some faults may exist but considers them insurable, implying that a title insurance provider is willing to back the title despite probable concerns.

Title insurance is critical in dealing with insurable titles, providing protection to both buyers and lenders against losses caused by title flaws that were not discovered during the title search. This covers hidden issues like forgery, fraud, and inaccuracies in public documents. Title insurance does not fix flaws, but it does give financial protection against claims or legal expenditures associated with defending the title.

Marketable vs. Insurable Title

The distinction between a marketable and an insurable title is that the latter accepts some flaws, provided they are covered by title insurance. While a marketable title is desirable, an insurable title is a feasible option that allows transactions to occur while financial precautions are in place.

Insurable titles are frequently used when flaws are discovered that are either too minor or too complex to be resolved promptly. In such instances, title insurance ensures that the sale can proceed, with the insurance provider bearing the risk of future claims against the property.

Anyone participating in real estate transactions should understand the distinction between marketable and insurable titles, as well as the procedures for verifying these requirements. While a clear, marketable title is always preferred, insurable titles provide a path to transaction completion when complications arise. Title insurance is important in this context because it provides a safety net against problems that could jeopardize property ownership and financial investment. The interplay of these ideas emphasizes the value of due diligence, professional guidance, and educated decision-making in real estate purchases. By carefully managing these factors, buyers, sellers, and professionals can ensure that property transfers are completed securely, protecting the interests of all parties involved and preserving the real estate market's integrity.

TYPES OF DEEDS

In the field of real estate, passing property ownership from one individual to another is a legal process that is primarily reliant on the document. A deed is a legally binding document that transfers ownership of property. It includes the names of the original and new owners, as well as a detailed description of the property. The significance of deeds in real estate transactions cannot be emphasized, as they not only register the transfer of ownership but also specify the terms and protections involved.

Understanding the various types of deeds is important because they allow the buyer to receive differing degrees of protection and warranties. The type of deed used in a property transaction can have a considerable impact on the security of the buyer's investment and the seller's obligations, ranging from ensuring clear title to providing no warranties.

1. General Warranty Deed: Among the different types of deeds, the General Warranty Deed stands out for offering the highest level of buyer protection. This deed makes comprehensive warranties or guarantees to the buyer about the title's quality and the property's ownership history.

A General Warranty Deed guarantees the customer that:

- The seller owns the property with clear title.
- The property is not subject to liens and encumbrances, save the ones specified in the deed.
- The buyer will enjoy quiet possession of the property, undisturbed by claims of ownership or outstanding legal issues from others.

These warranties are applicable throughout the property's history, not only during the seller's ownership. This component of the General Warranty Deed provides important peace of mind to the buyer by granting legal redress against the seller if any claims against the property's title arise after the transaction.

A General Warranty Deed is the favored choice for the majority of residential property purchases due to the extensive protection it provides. Buyers can proceed with trust, understanding that their ownership rights are completely safeguarded. For sellers, providing a General Warranty Deed can be a powerful selling factor, expressing their trust in the property's clear title and enhancing its marketability.

In essence, the General Warranty Deed is the gold standard in property conveyance, assuring that the transfer of ownership is supported by the most complete warranties about the title's integrity.

2. Special Warranty Deed: A Special Warranty Deed strikes a balance in terms of protection between the extensive assurance of a General Warranty Deed and the modest promises of a Quitclaim Deed. It's a popular instrument in commercial real estate transactions and instances where the seller can't fully verify the property's history.

A Special Warranty Deed, as opposed to a General Warranty Deed, extends only to the period when the property was owned by the seller. The seller assures that there have been no title flaws while their possession, but does not warrant against any issues that may have existed prior to that period.

This limited warranty makes the Special Warranty Deed particularly suitable for:

- Properties with frequent ownership changes or complex histories.
- Sellers who are confident in the state of the title during their ownership period but do not have comprehensive knowledge of the property's entire history.

The Special Warranty Deed offers a balance of protection and flexibility, allowing for the transfer of ownership with assurances that are tailored to the seller's knowledge and the property's specific circumstances.

3. Quitclaim Deed

The Quitclaim Deed is the most basic type of deed in real estate transactions, providing no assurances or guarantees on the property's title. It conveys the seller's (grantor's) interest in the property to the buyer (grantee) without saying whether or not that interest is genuine. Characteristics and Use:

- **No Warranties**: The Quitclaim Deed does not guarantee that the grantor has clear title or ownership of the property; it just transfers any interest the grantor may have.
- **Clearing Title Defects**: Often used in situations where the goal is to clear up title defects or ambiguities, as it can be a quick way to transfer rights without the formalities of other deeds.
- **Transfers Between Familiar Parties**: Commonly used for transfers between family members or into a trust, where the parties involved have a trusting relationship and do not need the formal protections of warranty deeds.

Given its lack of warranties, the Quitclaim Deed is generally not used in standard real estate sales, especially those involving financing, as lenders typically require assurance of clear title. Its primary function is in non-sale transactions where the precise nature of the title might not be clear but is not disputed between the parties involved.

4. Bargain and Sale Deed

4. Bargain and Sale Deed: The Bargain and Sale Deed is a specific type of deed that, while it conveys ownership of a property from the seller to the buyer, does so with a distinct set of characteristics that set it apart from other deeds.

- **Conveyance Without Warranties**: Much like the Quitclaim Deed, the Bargain and Sale Deed does not provide the buyer with any warranties against liens or other encumbrances on the property. It just transfers the seller's stake in the property to the purchaser.
- **Implication of Ownership**: Unlike the Quitclaim Deed, which does not necessarily imply any ownership interest in the property, the Bargain and Sale Deed implies that the seller has some ownership stake in the property. However, it does not guarantee that this interest is free of issues.

Specific Circumstances

- **Tax Sales**: This type of deed is commonly used in transactions involving tax sales, where a property is sold by the government to recover unpaid taxes. The government entity selling the property may not guarantee its condition or title status, making the Bargain and Sale Deed an appropriate instrument for such transactions.
- **Foreclosure Sales**: Similarly, properties sold through foreclosure may be conveyed via a Bargain and Sale Deed, where the seller (typically a bank or financial institution) implies ownership but does not provide warranties regarding the property's title.

5. Grant Deed

5. Grant Deed: The Grant Deed serves as a middle ground among types of deeds, offering more assurance than a Quitclaim or Bargain and Sale Deed, but less than a General Warranty Deed.

- **Guarantees Against Prior Conveyance**: One of the most important characteristics of a Grant Deed is the promise that the real estate has not been sold to anyone person. It guarantees that the grantor has not already transferred the real estate to another person.
- **Freedom from Undisclosed Encumbrances**: Additionally, the Grant Deed guarantees that, to the best of the seller's knowledge, the property is free from undisclosed liens or encumbrances. This does not cover issues unknown to the seller but offers moderate protection to the buyer against pre-existing claims.

Common Usage

- **Moderate Assurance Transactions**: In places where Grant Deeds are widespread, they are frequently used in residential property transactions where the seller may firmly allege no prior conveyance or known concealed encumbrances. It achieves a balance between the limited promises of a Quitclaim Deed and the broad warranties of a General Warranty Deed.
- **Legal Implications**: The use of a Grant Deed places a legal obligation on the seller regarding the assurances provided. If it is later revealed that there were unreported encumbrances or past conveyances, the buyer may have legal action against the seller under the promises made in the deed.

6. Deed of Trust: In the landscape of real estate financing, the Deed of Trust plays a pivotal role. A Deed of Trust, unlike a regular mortgage, is entered into by three parties: the lender, the borrower and a trustee. This document not only signifies the transfer of title but also secures the loan on the property.

The Three-Party System

- **Borrower**: The individual or entity receiving the loan and purchasing the property. In the context of a Deed of Trust, the borrower transfers the property title to the trustee as security for the loan.
- **Lender**: The financial institution or person making the loan. The lender's interest is preserved by the trustee, who maintains the property title until the financing is fully returned.
- **Trustee**: A neutral third party holding the property's title until the loan terms are satisfied. The trustee plays an important function since they have the power to foreclose on the property on the lender's behalf if the borrower does not repay the debt.

The Deed of Trust is published with the county, becoming a public record and officially establishing a lien on the property. This lien acts as collateral for the lender, ensuring that the loan is repaid or that the property can be foreclosed on and sold to pay the obligation.

The foreclosure procedure is one of the most defining elements of a Deed of Trust. If the borrower defaults, the trustee can start a non-judicial foreclosure, which is often faster than the judicial foreclosure process necessary for traditional mortgages. This method varies by state but usually involves less judicial participation, resulting in a faster settlement.

Conclusion

Understanding the various forms of deeds is essential for navigating the complexity of real estate transactions and financing. From the protective assurances of a General Warranty Deed to the specialized applications of a Bargain and Sale Deed, Grant Deed, or Deed of Trust in financing, each deed serves a unique purpose and provides varying levels of protection and obligations.

As we complete this discussion on deeds, it is evident that the choice of deed has substantial consequences for all parties engaged in a real estate transaction. Whether assuring clear title transfer, managing financing arrangements, or limiting risk, choosing the right deed is critical to successful and secure real estate transactions.

FEATURES OF A VALID DEED

A deed is an important legal document in real estate because it allows one party to transfer ownership of property to another. This document, which is essential to the conveyance process, must meet specific requirements in order to be regarded legitimate and effective in conveying a clear and undisputed title.

A genuine deed assures that the transaction follows legal requirements, offering security and peace of mind to both the seller (grantor) and the buyer (grantee). The significance of a legitimate deed cannot be emphasized, since it not only confirms the transfer of ownership but also influences the property's future marketability and the buyer's ability to obtain financing or sell it.

1. Legal Capacity of the Parties: For a deed to be legally binding, all parties involved—the grantor and the grantee—must have the legal capacity to enter into a contract. Legal capacity refers to the ability of a party to be bound by the terms of the contract, which includes understanding the nature and effect of the transaction.

- **Determining Legal Capacity**: This usually entails ensuring that the participants are of legal age and have a cognitive ability to comprehend the transaction. Corporations and other entities must have the authority under their organizational rules to engage in the transaction.
- **Significance**: The parties' legal competence is a necessary condition for the deed's legality. A deed executed by a party lacking legal capacity can be challenged, potentially rendering the transaction void or voidable, thus jeopardizing the security of the property transfer.

2. Intent to Convey Property: A legitimate deed must clearly indicate the grantor's intent to pass the property to the recipient. This intent must be unmistakably declared within the deed's provisions, leaving no doubt as to the purpose of the document.
- **Manifestation of Intent**: The deed must express the grantor's purpose to transfer ownership of the property listed in the instrument to the grantee. This is often achieved through specific language and terms used in the deed, such as "convey and warrant," which indicate the transfer of ownership.
- **Language and Structure**: The structure of the deed and the language used are carefully crafted to ensure that the intent to convey is clear and legally enforceable. Ambiguities or omissions in expressing this intent can lead to disputes over the deed's validity and, consequently, the legality of the property transfer.

3. Adequate Property Description: To be lawful, a deed must contain an appropriate description of the property being conveyed. This condition assures that the attribute can be clearly identified based on the description alone, without the need for additional evidence. An precise property description is critical for avoiding disputes over whether land is included in the sale. Methods of Property Description
- **Metes and Bounds**: This method describes property boundaries using reference points, distances, and angles. Metes refer to the measurement of the boundary lines (often in feet), while bounds refer to the boundary lines' direction. This method is one of the most precise but can be complex.
- **Lot and Block**: Common in residential developments, this method refers to property by its lot and block number within a recorded subdivision plat. It is simpler and relies on the plat map filed in public records to provide detailed boundary descriptions.
- **Rectangular Survey System**: This approach, often called the Public Land Survey System (PLSS), divides land into townships and sections. It's used primarily in the Western United States and provides a standardized way to describe large parcels of land.
- **Reference to Public Records**: Sometimes, property descriptions refer to documents recorded in public records, such as earlier deeds or official surveys, to describe the property.

Inaccuracies or ambiguities in the property description can lead to legal disputes over boundary lines or the extent of the property conveyed. A valid deed requires a clear description that corresponds to the actual and legal reality of the property.

4. Consideration: Consideration in a deed refers to something of value transferred between the two parties as a component of the property transfer. While the traditional view of consideration involves monetary payment, the law recognizes various forms of consideration in real estate transactions. Role in Validating a Deed:
- **Monetary Payment**: The most common form of consideration, involving a specific amount of money the grantee agrees to pay the grantor.
- **Other Forms of Value**: Consideration can also include other valuable exchanges, such as other property, services, or an assumption of debt. The key is that there is a mutual exchange of value that forms the basis of the agreement to transfer property.

Types of Consideration Recognized
- **Nominal Consideration**: Sometimes, deeds state a nominal consideration (e.g., "$10 and other valuable considerations") to fulfill legal requirements, even when the actual consideration is not specified or is non-monetary.
- **Good Consideration**: This can include natural love and affection in transfers between family members. While it may not have economic value, it is recognized as valid consideration for the purpose of deed validation.

5. Signature of the Grantor: One of the most critical features of a valid deed is the signature of the grantor, the party transferring the property. This signature is a legal affirmation that the grantor intends to convey the property described in the deed to the grantee. Jurisdictional Requirements:

- The specifics regarding the signature can vary by jurisdiction. Most jurisdictions require the grantor's signature to be witnessed, typically by one or two disinterested parties, and notarized by a commissioned notary public.
- Notarization acts as an additional layer of verification, confirming the identity of the grantor and their voluntary act of signing. This approach helps to prevent fraud and ensures the deed's integrity.

The Role of Witnesses and Notarization

- Witnesses and notarization serve to validate the authenticity of the signature, providing a legal safeguard against disputes over the deed's execution.
- In some jurisdictions, the lack of required witnesses or notarization can render a deed invalid or, at least, complicate the process of proving its validity if challenged.

6. Delivery and Acceptance: For a deed to effectively transfer property ownership, it must not only be executed correctly but also be delivered to and accepted by the grantee. Delivery and acceptance are crucial components that finalize the transfer process. Delivery of the Deed:

- Delivery refers to the grantor's intention to make the deed operative immediately, relinquishing control over the document (and thus the property) to the grantee.
- Physical delivery of the deed is the most straightforward method, but symbolic or constructive delivery, where actions or words indicate the grantor's intention to transfer the property, can also suffice.

Acceptance by the Grantee

- Acceptance occurs when the grantee agrees to take the deed, thereby accepting the transfer of property. Acceptance is usually presumed if the transfer benefits the grantee.
- The process of acceptance underscores the transaction's consensual nature, ensuring that the property transfer is mutually agreed upon.

Conclusion

The attributes of a valid deed serve as the foundation for real estate property transmission. Each aspect is critical to maintaining the deed's legitimacy and efficacy, as well as protecting the grantor's and grantee's rights.

Understanding these elements is critical for anybody involved in real estate transactions because they determine the deed's capacity to perform its principal function: the unambiguous and undisputed transfer of property ownership. Ensuring that a deed is properly executed, given, and accepted helps to avoid future problems by giving clarity and security for property ownership.

GUARANTEES FOR HOMEOWNERS

In the complex world of real estate transactions, guarantees are critical to protecting homeowners' interests and investments. These assurances, which are supplied through various legal procedures, provide an additional layer of protection and peace of mind, allowing homeowners to enjoy their property without fear of unanticipated legal entanglements or encumbrances. Understanding these guarantees is critical for anyone entering into a real estate transaction, since they have a direct impact on the legitimacy and safety of their investment in property.

For homeowners, assurances are more than just legal formalities; they are the foundation of property ownership confidence. These safeguards protect against future disputes or claims that could jeopardize the homeowner's title to the property, potentially resulting in financial loss or legal action. In essence, guarantees assure that homeowners can fully exercise their rights to use, enjoy, and finally sell their property without encountering any unexpected claims or liens.

Title Insurance as a Guarantee

Among the different types of homeowner guarantees, title insurance stands out as an essential safeguard. This specialty insurance product is intended to protect homeowners (and their lenders) from potential losses caused by problems in the title to the property. Owner's and Lender's Policies:

- **Owner's Policy**: Protects the homeowner against title issues that may surface after the purchase, covering legal fees and losses up to the value of the insurance.
- **Lender's Policy**: This policy, which is typically needed by mortgage lenders, safeguards the lender's interest in the real estate as long as the mortgage is paid off in full.

Title insurance is unique in that it provides retrospective coverage, protecting against concerns that existed before the insurance was acquired but were discovered after. It is a one-time purchase made at closing that will remain in effect as long as the homeowner or their heirs possess the property.

Types of Title Insurance Coverage

Title insurance policies come in various forms, offering different levels of protection based on the homeowner's needs and the property's specific risks.

1. Standard Coverage: Standard title insurance policies cover a range of common issues that might affect a property's title, including:

- **Forgery and Fraud**: Protection against loss due to forged documents or fraudulent transactions.
- **Encroachments**: Coverage if another building or structure encroaches onto the insured property.
- **Undisclosed Heirs**: Protection against claims by previously unknown heirs of former owners.

2. Enhanced Coverage: For additional protection, homeowners can opt for enhanced title insurance policies that cover more complex issues, such as:

- **Zoning Issues**: Coverage for losses due to certain zoning law violations.
- **Structural Damage**: Protection against structural damage from improper subdivision, building permits, or mineral extraction.

Enhanced plans provide broader coverage by addressing more specific and possibly costly hazards that ordinary policies may not cover. Homeowners should carefully examine their property's particular dangers and speak with a title insurance professional to determine the best level of coverage.

Warranties in Real Estate Transactions

Warranties are essential components of real estate transactions, providing homeowners with additional levels of security and assurance about the status and condition of their property. These guarantees are often transmitted by warranty deeds at closing, protecting the buyer from certain flaws or concerns with the property title.

General Warranty Deeds vs. Special Warranty Deeds

- **General Warranty Deeds** provide the most comprehensive level of protection. They guarantee the buyer against any title problems or claims that might arise, covering the entire history of the property. The seller commits to addressing any such claims and ensuring the buyer's peaceful and undisputed ownership.
- **Special Warranty Deeds**, on the other hand, offer a more limited assurance. The seller only guarantees against issues or claims that occurred under their possession. This means that any problems from before the seller's ownership period may not be covered under this deed type.

These warranties play an important role in providing homeowners with piece of mind by ensuring the legal status of their property and protecting them from potential future conflicts.

Covenants in deeds can serve as long-term guarantees for homeowners by dictating the usage, limits, and rights associated with a property. These legally enforceable commitments ensure that specific property-related conditions be met by both the current and future owners.

Common Covenants
- Restrictive Covenants limit how a property can be used, which can include limitations on the type of structures that can be built or prohibitions on commercial use in a residential area.
- Maintenance Covenants require the property owner to maintain the property to a certain standard, often used in communities with homeowners' associations to ensure a uniform appearance and upkeep of properties.

Covenants can significantly impact how homeowners enjoy their property and their responsibilities towards it, influencing the property's value and appeal.

Ensuring Guarantees Are Upheld
For homeowners, ensuring that the guarantees provided by warranties and covenants are upheld is paramount to protecting their investment and interests.
- **Legal Advice and Due Diligence**: Engaging legal specialists to analyze and advise on the implications of warranties and covenants is critical. This ensures that homeowners are fully aware of their rights and obligations under these promises.
- **Title Insurance**: Obtaining title insurance adds an extra layer of protection by covering potential concerns that are not covered by the deed's warranties. It's a critical step in safeguarding against unforeseen claims or legal challenges.

Guarantees for homeowners, whether through deeds, covenants, or title insurance, are critical to assuring the security and enjoyment of their property. They give a structure for homeowners to negotiate their rights and responsibilities while also protecting them from potential future legal entanglements. Understanding and securing these guarantees at the time of property acquisition is critical, necessitating extensive due diligence and, in many cases, competent legal advice. This proactive approach guarantees that homeowners may completely enjoy their property, knowing that it is legally sound and that they can handle any concerns that may occur.

FINALIZING THE TRANSFER OF REAL ESTATE

The last stage of a real estate transaction—the moment when ownership of a property transfers from the seller to the buyer—is characterized by rigorous coordination and painstaking attention to detail. This final phase, which is crucial for guaranteeing a legal and secure transfer of ownership, entails numerous key actions and documentation. To avoid future disagreements or legal concerns over property ownership, it is necessary to be detailed and accurate.

Execution of the Deed
The execution of the deed is a pivotal moment in the transfer of real estate. Once signed by all parties concerned, this legal document officially conveys ownership of the real estate from the seller (grantor) to the buyer. Necessary Signatures and Notarization:
- **Signatures**: The deed must be signed by the grantor, with some jurisdictions also requiring the grantee's signature. These signatures serve as a formal acknowledgement of the transfer and the terms outlined in the deed.
- **Notarization**: A notary public typically witnesses the signing of the deed, providing an additional layer of verification. Notarization certifies the signers' identification and the authenticity of their signatures, making the document legally enforceable.

The deed serves as more than simply a record of the transaction; it is also the legal instrument that transfers property ownership. It must accurately identify the property, state the consideration (if applicable), and clarify any terms or warranties attached to the transaction.

Closing Process
The closing process represents the transaction's final stage, where all documents are signed, and ownership officially changes hands. Key Documents and Agreements:

- **Loan Documents**: For transactions involving financing, the buyer signs a mortgage or deed of trust, along with a promissory note agreeing to the loan terms.
- **Title Documents**: The deed and any documents clarifying the property's title are signed and reviewed.
- **Settlement Statement**: A document detailing the financial transactions involved in the closing, including sales price, loan amounts, and closing costs.

Recording the Deed

Recording the deed with the local government's office is an important step in completing the transfer of real estate. This public recording:

- **Protects the Buyer's Ownership Rights**: Recording the deed gives notice to the world of the buyer's ownership, helping to protect against fraudulent claims against the property.
- **Varied Requirements and Fees**: The process for recording a deed varies by jurisdiction, including differences in required documentation, fees, and timing. Prompt recording is essential to safeguard the buyer's interests.

Settlement Statement

The settlement statement, which includes the financial facts of the transaction, is crucial to concluding the transfer of real estate. It is the financial "receipt" of the closing process, listing both the buyer's and seller's fees, payments, and credits.

HUD-1 and Closing Disclosure

- **HUD-1**: The HUD-1 Settlement Statement, which is traditionally used in closings involving federally connected mortgage loans, includes all expenses and credits incurred by the buyer and seller during the transaction. Although its use has waned, it remains relevant in some types of real estate transactions.
- **Closing Disclosure**: The Closing Disclosure has become the standard form for most mortgage-financed residential property purchases. It contains information about the mortgage loan, such as the loan terms, expected monthly payments, and closing fees related with the property purchase.

Role of the Settlement Statement

- **Transparency**: The settlement statement promotes transparency by allowing both parties to view a thorough analysis of expenses and changes. This transparency helps to avoid surprises at closure and ensures that all parties agree on the financial conditions of the transaction.
- **Record Keeping**: It also serves as an essential record for future reference, useful for tax purposes, financial planning, and resolving any post-closing disputes that might arise.

Title Insurance Update

With the property officially transferred, updating title insurance is a crucial step in protecting the new ownership status against past undiscovered or undisclosed issues. Importance for the Buyer:

- **Protection Against Past Issues**: An updated title insurance policy ensures the buyer is protected against potential title defects that weren't identified during the initial title search, including forgery, undisclosed heirs, or errors in public records.
- **Ensuring Peace of Mind**: Having an updated title insurance policy in place gives you piece of mind knowing that your investment is protected against legal and financial losses due to title issues.

Process for Obtaining Updated Policy

- **Contact the Title Insurance Company**: The buyer or their legal representative should contact the company that issued the original title insurance policy to request an update reflecting the new ownership.
- **Review and Adjustment**: The title insurance company may conduct an additional review of the title and adjust the coverage based on any new developments or findings since the initial policy issuance.
- **Issuance of New Policy**: Once the review is complete and any necessary adjustments are made, the title insurance company will issue an updated policy to the new homeowner, ensuring continuous protection.

Finalizing the transfer of real estate is a multidimensional process that requires thorough attention to legal, financial, and administrative elements. From the careful writing and recording of the deed to the precise accounting supplied by the settlement statement, every step is intended to provide a transparent, equitable, and secure transfer of property ownership. Updating title insurance after closing strengthens the deal and protects the new homeowner from unexpected title concerns. The completion of these steps not only concludes a real estate transaction, but also signals the start of a new chapter for the homeowner. Understanding and effectively handling these last phases will allow all parties involved to have a successful and fulfilling real estate journey.

ESTIMATING SETTLEMENT EXPENSES

In the final phases of a real estate transaction, both purchasers and sellers face a variety of settlement expenses—costs that are in addition to the purchase or selling price and are required to formally finish the deal. Understanding these fees is critical because they have a substantial impact on the entire financial outlay associated with transferring property ownership. Settlement expenses include a variety of fees and charges that all contribute to the legal, administrative, and financial needs of closing a real estate transaction. Both parties rely heavily on accurate cost estimates. For purchasers, it assures that adequate funds are available to complete the transaction; for sellers, it clarifies the net revenues of the sale. The process of closing a real estate purchase entails a slew of financial commitments, some expected and others unexpected.

1. Closing Costs

- *Loan Origination Fees*: The lender will require costs to process the new loan.
- *Appraisal Fees*: Costs associated with evaluating the property's value.
- *Title Searches and Title Insurance*: Fees for verifying the title's validity and insuring against potential title issues.
- *Surveys*: Expenses for verifying property boundaries.
- *Taxes and Deed Recording Fees*: Government charges for recording the new deed.
- *Credit Report Charges*: Fees for accessing the buyer's credit history during the loan approval procedure.

2. Attorney Fees: Legal representation during a real estate transaction ensures that all documents are correctly prepared and filed. Attorney fees cover the expense of legal representation, which can differ subject to the details and geography.

3. Prepaid Expenses: Some expenses must be paid upfront at closing, including:

- *Property Taxes*: Prorated taxes the buyer owes upon taking ownership.
- *Homeowners Insurance*: Advance payment on the property's insurance policy.
- *Mortgage Interest*: Interest that accrues between the closing date and the first mortgage payment.

4. Escrow Accounts: Lenders often require the creation of escrow accounts to cover future payments of property taxes and homeowners insurance. A portion of these costs is collected at closing to fund the account initially.

Calculating Settlement Expenses

Estimating settlement expenses entails analyzing each potential cost and determining how it applies to the particular transaction. Online calculators can provide preliminary estimates, but working with professionals—attorneys and lenders—is essential for obtaining exact data.

Negotiations about who bears what settlement expenditures can have a substantial impact on the transaction's financial dynamics. Buyers and sellers can negotiate these fees as part of the entire agreement, with some charges being paid by one party rather than the other.

Understanding and preparing for settlement fees ensures that the closing day is free of financial shocks, enabling both parties to enjoy the exhilaration of transferring property ownership.

Negotiating Settlement Expenses

The negotiation of settlement expenses is critical to the entire financial picture of a real estate transaction. These costs, often substantial, can be a point of discussion and compromise between the buyer and seller. Strategies for Negotiation:

- **Seller Concessions**: Sellers may offer to cover certain costs as a concession to make the sale more appealing or to expedite the process. This can be particularly effective in buyers' markets, where sellers are motivated to close the deal.
- **Closing Cost Credits**: Both parties may agree on closing cost credits, where the seller agrees to a higher purchase price, provided they cover specific closing costs for the buyer. This can be advantageous for customers with limited upfront cash.
- **Dividing Costs Equitably**: Some expenses, like transfer taxes or association fees, can be split between the buyer and seller. This equitable division can be negotiated based on the norms in the local real estate market.

Leveraging Expenses in Negotiations
- **Strategic Use of Expenses**: Buyers can use the willingness to absorb certain costs as a negotiation tool to lower the overall purchase price or secure concessions in other areas.
- **Understanding Market Conditions**: Knowledge of local market conditions can empower either party in negotiations. For example, in a seller's market, buyers might be more willing to take on additional costs to secure their desired property.

Preparing for Settlement Day
Settlement day symbolizes the end of the real estate purchase process, when the seller formally transfers ownership to the buyer. Adequate preparation ensures a smooth and stress-free closing.

1. Arranging Necessary Funds
- **Review the Closing Disclosure**: Buyers should carefully review the Closing Disclosure (or HUD-1 Settlement Statement) provided by the lender. This document outlines all the costs due at closing, allowing buyers to arrange for the necessary funds.
- **Securing Payment Methods**: Ensure that the money are easily available. This often means arranging a wire transfer or obtaining a cashier's check in advance of the closing date.

2. Understanding the Settlement Statement
- **Itemization of Costs**: The settlement statement contains a full summary of all transaction costs, including both buyer and seller charges. Reviewing this contract helps both parties understand their financial commitments and ensures that all charges are properly accounted for.
- **Finalizing Expenses**: Any discrepancies or questions regarding the listed expenses should be addressed before settlement day. This includes confirming that all negotiated credits or concessions are accurately reflected.

To successfully complete the chapter on estimating settlement expenses, you must first grasp the negotiation methods and preparation processes necessary for settlement day. Buyers and sellers might both benefit financially from effectively negotiating settlement expenses. Preparing for settlement day by providing sufficient cash and properly comprehending the settlement statement ensures that the closing process goes smoothly, resulting in a successful real estate transaction. This complete approach to managing settlement fees not only makes the transaction go more smoothly, but it also helps to ensure a clear and equitable transfer of property ownership.

TAXES ON REAL ESTATE OWNERSHIP

R eal estate taxes play an important part in property ownership, intertwining with property owners' financial duties and contributions to their communities. These taxes, imposed by local and state governments, are a fundamental component of the public funding paradigm, influencing the delivery of basic services and infrastructure development.

Role in Property Ownership
- Real estate taxes are recurring financial obligations tied to the ownership of property, varying significantly based on location, property value, and local tax policies.
- They serve as a key source of revenue for local governments, directly influencing the quality and availability of public services within communities.

Contribution to Local and State Revenues
- The funds collected from real estate taxes are allocated to a wide range of services that benefit the community, including public education, emergency services, public parks, road maintenance, and more.
- This taxation system ensures that property owners contribute to the maintenance and development of the infrastructure and services they utilize.

Property taxes constitute the majority of real estate-related tax obligations, directly impacting homeowners and property investors alike. Calculation of Property Taxes:
- Property taxes are determined by assessing the property's value and applying the local tax rate. Assessments are conducted by local government officials and are meant to reflect the property's current market value.
- Understanding the local tax structure is crucial for property owners, as tax rates can vary significantly among jurisdictions.

Transfer Taxes
The transfer of property ownership results in another type of taxation known as transfer taxes. These taxes are levied when a property's title passes from one proprietor to another. Transfer taxes are computed as a proportion of the property's sale price or assessed value, depending on the jurisdiction's regulations. While these fees are typically the responsibility of the seller, bargaining throughout the selling process might result in the buyer sharing or assuming them, impacting the overall cost of the transaction.

Variations Across Jurisdictions
- Transfer tax rates can significantly differ from one location to another, with some areas imposing higher rates than others. This variety makes understanding local tax rules a vital element of the property transaction process.
- Certain jurisdictions may provide exemptions or lower fees for transactions between family members or first-time homeowners.

Capital Gains Taxes
When a real estate asset is sold for more than its purchase price, the profit earned constitutes a capital gain, which is subject to capital gains taxes. This tax is a significant consideration for property sellers, as it directly impacts the net proceeds from the sale. Mitigating Capital Gains Tax:
- **Primary Residence Exclusion**: Homeowners may subtract up to $250,000 ($500,000 for married couples filing jointly) in capital gains tax if they utilized the property as their main place of residence for a minimum of two of the five years before the sale.
- **Real Estate Investment Strategies**: For investment properties, procedures such as a 1031 exchange can delay capital gains taxes by reinvesting the proceeds in another investment property within a set time frame.

Understanding the implications of capital gains taxes and the available strategies to mitigate them is crucial for property sellers to maximize their profits and make informed decisions about their real estate investments.

Special Assessments

Special assessment taxes are additional charges levied on real estate owners for projects that directly benefit their property or community, such as infrastructure improvements or public utility upgrades. Determination and Billing:

- **Assessment Process**: Local governments or homeowners' associations typically determine the need for special assessments. The cost is then divided among the benefiting properties, often based on frontage, square footage, or other relevant metrics.
- **Billing and Payment**: Special assessments can be billed as a lump sum or spread out over several years. Property owners should be aware of these potential costs and plan accordingly, as these assessments can significantly impact annual property expenses.

Effective management of real estate tax obligations necessitates strategic planning and an awareness of the tax environment. Property owners should incorporate annual property taxes in their budgets. Setting away monies on a monthly basis will help reduce the financial pressure when taxes are due. Examine property tax bills carefully for errors in assessment or exemptions that may lower the tax liability. Escrow accounts are frequently established by lenders to collect and manage property tax and insurance payments for mortgaged homeowners. These accounts ensure that taxes and insurance are paid on time, avoiding penalties and keeping coverage.

Real estate taxes cover a wide range of requirements, including property and transfer taxes, capital gains, and special assessments. Each of these taxes has repercussions for property owners, influencing their financial planning and investment outcomes. Property owners can ensure they are prepared for their fiscal responsibilities by implementing measures to reduce tax liabilities and effectively manage tax obligations, thereby contributing to their financial stability and the long-term value of their real estate investments.

DUTIES ON PROPERTY CONVEYANCE

The conveyance of property, a vital element in real estate transactions, comprises transferring title from the seller to the buyer. This process is governed by a complex interplay of legal and procedural responsibilities, which ensures that the transfer is carried out legitimately and transparently. For both parties involved—the seller (grantor) and the buyer (grantee), a clear understanding of these obligations is critical to a seamless transaction.

Conveyance duties include a wide range of responsibilities, from verifying the clear ownership of the property to appropriately disclosing property conditions. These obligations are intended to protect both parties' interests by establishing a framework within which the transfer of ownership can take place without disagreements or unexpected issues.

Seller's Duties

1. Clear Title Provision: One of the most important tasks of the seller in the property conveyance process is to offer a clear and marketable title. This means there are no liens, encumbrances, or legal conflicts that could jeopardize the buyer's ability to secure and enjoy full ownership.

- **Title Searches**: To meet this responsibility, sellers frequently undertake a title search, which is a review of public documents to confirm the property's legal ownership and uncover any concerns.
- **Resolving Title Issues**: If any title concerns are detected, it is the seller's responsibility to resolve them before the transfer can proceed. This might involve paying off liens or addressing disputes.

2. Accurate Property Disclosure: Sellers are additionally obligated to share any known faults or concerns with the real estate. This requirement is not only a legal obligation in many jurisdictions, but also an issue of ethical responsibility during the sales process.

- **Disclosure Forms**: These disclosures are typically made through formal disclosure forms, where sellers list any known problems with the property, ranging from structural issues to history of flood damage.
- **Importance of Transparency**: Accurate disclosure helps prevent future disputes and claims, ensuring the buyer

is fully informed about the property's condition before the purchase.

3. Compliance with Contract Terms: Ensuring that all conditions and terms outlined in the sale contract are met is another critical duty of the seller.

- **Sale Inclusions and Exclusions**: This includes adhering to agreed-upon terms regarding what is included or excluded from the sale, such as appliances, fixtures, or other personal property.
- **Contractual Obligations**: Sellers must also ensure that any other contractual obligations, such as agreed repairs or modifications to the property, are completed prior to closing.

Buyer's Duties

1. Due Diligence in Property Inspection: Buyers must do rigorous due diligence, particularly on property inspections. This proactive stage is critical for identifying any hidden faults or possible problems with the property that are not immediately evident or reported.

- **Professional Inspections**: It is normal practice to hire expert inspectors to analyze the property's condition, which includes structural integrity, electrical systems, plumbing, and other factors. These inspections can discover issues that could have a significant influence on the property's value or result in costly repairs after the sale.
- **Reviewing Disclosures**: In addition to inspections, buyers should carefully evaluate any disclosures provided by the seller, comparing revealed faults to inspection findings to ensure a thorough understanding of the property's state.

2. Securing Financing: Another critical duty for many buyers is securing financing for their property purchase. This involves obtaining a mortgage or other loan, a process that entails its own set of responsibilities and requirements.

- **Mortgage Approval**: Buyers must navigate the mortgage application process, which includes providing financial documents, undergoing credit checks, and meeting specific lender criteria to obtain loan approval.
- **Loan Conditions**: Adhering to the conditions of the loan is vital. This can include maintaining a certain credit score, ensuring the property meets the lender's standards (via an appraisal), and finalizing all necessary paperwork.

3. Closing Preparation: Preparing for the closing process involves several key responsibilities for the buyer, aimed at ensuring all financial and legal aspects are in order for the transfer of ownership.

- **Understanding Settlement Expenses**: Buyers should familiarize themselves with the expected settlement expenses, detailed in the settlement statement or Closing Disclosure. This includes closing costs, prepaid expenses, and adjustments.
- **Arranging Funds**: Ensuring the necessary funds are available for closing is essential. This often means securing a cashier's check or arranging a wire transfer for the total amount due at closing, including down payment and closing costs.

Conclusion

The duties of property conveyance establish a framework of responsibilities for both sellers and buyers, including legal, financial, and procedural factors. Sellers must provide clear titles, provide truthful disclosures, and conform with contractual obligations. For buyers, completing comprehensive inspections, obtaining financing, and preparing for closing are critical steps in protecting their investment. Together, these responsibilities promote a transparent, equitable, and efficient procedure, providing the framework for a smooth transfer of property ownership.

CHAPTER 10 – FOUNDAMENTALS OF REAL ESTATE PRACTICE

ESCROW ACCOUNT IN REAL ESTATE TRANSACTIONS

Escrow accounts play an important role in real estate transactions, serving as a neutral third-party mediator who keeps assets—such as money, property deeds, or other documents—until the terms of a real estate agreement are met. This strategy boosts confidence and security by ensuring that each of the buyer and seller execute their responsibilities before the deal is finalized.

- **Definition**: An escrow account is an economic agreement in which an external party keeps and manages the payment of funds requested by two parties in a transaction. It improves transaction security by maintaining the money in a secure escrow account, which becomes available when all of the requirements of a contract are met, as supervised by the escrow company.
- **Role in Real Estate Transactions**: Escrow accounts minimize the risk of a real estate transaction by acting as a safeguard, ensuring that the buyer's funds are available for the purchase and the seller's property is as agreed upon.

The escrow process is a critical component of a real estate transaction, providing a systematic approach to ensuring the fair and secure exchange of property. Steps of the Escrow Process:

- **Opening an Escrow Account**: Once a buyer and seller agree on the sale terms, an escrow account is opened with a chosen escrow agent, typically a title company or an attorney specializing in real estate.
- **Roles and Responsibilities**: The escrow agent's duties include holding the buyer's deposit, ensuring the terms of the sale agreement are met, managing the documents related to the property transfer, and distributing funds according to the agreement.

Escrow accounts serve multiple functions in real estate transactions, including holding down payments and managing ongoing property-related expenses.

- **Holding Down Payments**: The buyer's down payment is frequently placed in an escrow account at the start of the sale process. This secures the cash until the sale is completed, guaranteeing that the deposit is only given to the seller if all selling conditions are met.
- **Property Expense Payments**: Escrow accounts are also used to manage recurring property-related expenses like property taxes and homeowners insurance. Lenders frequently need an escrow account from homeowners with mortgages to guarantee that these expenses are paid on time, reducing delinquencies and keeping the property insured and tax-compliant.

Process for Establishing an Escrow Account

- **Selection of an Escrow Agent**: The first step is to select a competent and neutral third party to function as the escrow agent. This could be a title company, a real estate-focused law firm, or a bank. The agent's neutrality is critical to ensuring impartiality throughout the transaction.
- **Determining the Terms of the Escrow Agreement**: The buyer and seller have to mutually agree on the escrow account's precise parameters. These terms include the conditions under which the funds will be released and how disputes will be resolved.

Choosing a neutral third party as the escrow agent is critical to ensure the transaction is fair and impartial. This impartiality helps to avoid conflicts of interest and guarantees that the escrow agent acts in the best interests of both parties while strictly adhering to the agreed-upon parameters.

Protection for All Parties

Escrow accounts offer several advantages in real estate transactions, serving as a protective measure for all involved parties.

- **For Buyers**: Escrow accounts provide a security layer by holding the down payment and ensuring that the property title and other necessary documents are in order before the transaction is finalized.
- **For Sellers**: Sellers are assured that the buyer's funds are secured and will be released only upon the fulfillment of all sale conditions.
- **For Lenders**: Escrow accounts safeguard lenders by guaranteeing that property taxes and insurance premiums are settled on time, preserving the value of the collateral.

Escrow accounts make real estate transactions go more smoothly and efficiently by centralizing the collecting, storage, and disbursement of monies and crucial documents. This efficiency benefits all parties by lowering the possibility of delays and miscommunications.

Common Issues and Resolutions

Despite the safeguards provided by escrow accounts, problems might develop, demanding specific plans for resolution. Disputes over the release of funds or the handling of documents may arise. Such concerns are often resolved by open communication and adherence to the escrow agreement's conditions.

- **Effective Communication**: Maintaining open lines of communication among the buyer, seller, and escrow agent can assist in rapidly identifying and addressing any issues.
- **Legal Guidance**: Consulting with legal professionals can provide clarity and direction in resolving disputes, ensuring that the resolution complies with the escrow agreement and applicable laws.

Escrow accounts are critical to the integrity and seamless operation of real estate transactions, providing necessary safeguards and efficiencies. Understanding the process of opening an escrow account, the benefits it offers, and tactics for dealing with frequent concerns allows all parties to negotiate the complexity of real estate transactions with greater confidence and security.

UNACCEPTABLE PRACTICES IN REAL ESTATE

The real estate sector, which is a vital part of a community's economic and social fabric, is built on trust and integrity. Unethical real estate operations not only violate this fundamental trust, but also do enormous harm to individuals and communities, jeopardizing the industry's integrity and the larger societal fabric. Unethical behavior can range from purposeful misrepresentation to discriminating tactics, each with its own set of implications for the market and its participants.

The Impact of Unethical Practices

- **Individual Impact**: Unethical practices can lead directly to financial loss, emotional distress, and an unjust housing market for individuals. Buyers and sellers may find themselves in disadvantageous positions, manipulated by misinformation or discriminatory practices.
- **Community Impact**: Beyond individual consequences, unethical practices in real estate can contribute to wider community issues, such as segregation, diminished property values, and eroded trust in the housing market.
- **Market Integrity**: The prevalence of unethical behavior tarnishes the reputation of the real estate industry, potentially deterring honest transactions and fostering an environment of skepticism and litigation.

1. Blockbusting, a term coined in the mid-twentieth century, refers to the unethical practice of real estate brokers and others inducing residents to sell their properties at reduced rates by exploiting fears that racial, ethnic, or social changes in the neighborhood might harm property values. Mechanisms of Blockbusting:

- Exploiting Fears: Agents might spread rumors or exaggerate claims about demographic changes in a neighborhood to incite unfounded fears among homeowners.

- Undermining Property Values: By convincing homeowners that their property values will soon plummet, agents pressure them into selling at lower prices, often leading to significant financial loss.

Blockbusting began as a prevalent practice in the United States during the Great Migration, as African American families moved into largely white communities, causing racial tensions exploited by unscrupulous agents. In reaction to blockbusting and other similar activities, laws and regulations were developed, including the Fair Housing Act of 1968, to protect homeowners and assure equal treatment for all, regardless of race, religion, or nationality. Violations of these rules result in serious penalties, including fines and jail, demonstrating the legal system's dedication to eliminating such activities.

Blockbusting not only destabilizes neighborhoods, adds to segregation, and lowers property prices, but it also violates the real estate industry's ethical norms. Legal frameworks designed to counteract blockbusting reflect a broader public rejection of these activities, as well as a dedication to maintaining the housing market's integrity and fairness.

2. In real estate, steering is the process of manipulating buyer selections by directing them towards or away from specific communities based on discriminatory factors such as race, religion, or socioeconomic position. This manipulation not only violates the buyer's freedom to select freely, but it also reinforces segregation and inequality within communities.

- **Limiting Choices**: Agents might provide information or show properties only in certain areas, subtly guiding buyers based on biased perceptions or prejudices rather than the buyer's preferences or financial capabilities.
- **Impact on Buyers**: Buyers may be steered away from neighborhoods that offer better opportunities or value, limiting their choices and affecting their decision-making process.

Steering is forbidden by the Fair Housing Act, which seeks to eradicate discrimination in housing-related activities. Engaging in guiding techniques may result in legal implications, such as penalties and license revocation. By sustaining segregation, guiding leads to the deterioration of neighborhood variety and the widening of social differences, impeding efforts to promote inclusivity and equality in housing.

3. Redlining is a discriminatory practice in which lenders refuse or limit loans, mortgages, insurance, or other financial services in certain geographic areas, frequently based on racial or ethnic makeup. This practice, which began in the 1930s, routinely denied minority people access to critical financial services, adding to economic inequities and impeding community development.

- **Origins**: The term "redlining" derives from the red lines drawn on maps by lenders to delineate areas deemed high risk, primarily due to the racial composition of their residents, rather than objective financial criteria.
- **Effects on Neighborhoods**: Redlining has led to underinvestment in affected communities, resulting in diminished property values, inadequate infrastructure, and a lack of economic opportunities.

The Fair Housing Act and the Community Reinvestment Act were enacted to combat redlining and encourage equitable financing practices. These policies aim to ensure that everyone, regardless of race or ethnicity, has equal access to loans and financial services. Despite these regulations, the legacy of redlining remains, needing ongoing vigilance and enforcement efforts to deconstruct its long-term impacts and ensure fair access to financial services.

Truth in Advertising in Real Estate

In the competitive world of real estate, the integrity of advertising practices is paramount. Truth in advertising is not just an ethical obligation; it's a legal requirement designed to protect consumers from misleading or deceptive claims.

- **Importance**: The essence of truth in advertising is to provide potential buyers with accurate and clear information about properties, allowing them to make informed decisions.
- **Misleading Practices**: Examples include overstating the size or condition of a property, omitting significant property flaws, or presenting digitally altered images that misrepresent the property's appearance.

Various laws and regulations, such as the Federal Trade Commission (FTC) rules in the United States, establish criteria for truthful advertising, mandating that claims about properties be proven and not misleading. Violations can have serious implications, including penalties, legal action, and damage to professional reputations, stressing the importance of adhering to ethical advertising norms. The responsibility to avoid unethical activity in real estate extends beyond individual agents to the industry as a whole. Establishing and upholding strong ethical standards is critical to ensuring fairness and integrity in the housing industry.

Role of Real Estate Professionals
- **Upholding Standards**: Professionals across the industry, from agents to brokers and lenders, must commit to ethical conduct, actively working to prevent practices like blockbusting, steering, and redlining.
- **Continuous Education**: Ongoing training and education on ethical standards and legal requirements are essential for keeping professionals informed and vigilant against unethical practices.

Unacceptable real estate activities, such as blockbusting, guiding, redlining, and deceptive advertising, not only weaken the industry's ethical basis but also cause harm to individuals and communities. Combating these abuses necessitates a collaborative effort from all industry participants, emphasizing the need of ethical behavior, transparency, and accountability. By encouraging ethical behavior, the real estate business can promote a fair, inclusive, and trustworthy market for all.

ANTITRUST LAWS

Antitrust laws, which are essential for maintaining market competition and fairness, serve as the foundation for ethical business practices in a variety of industries, including real estate. These laws are intended to protect consumers and businesses against unfair competition and monopolistic actions that may undermine economic fairness and innovation.

Antitrust laws are basically created to prevent monopolies and encourage competition in the business sector. They outlaw actions deemed harmful to customers, such as price fixing, monopolization, and other anti-competitive tactics. The Sherman Antitrust Act, passed in 1890, signaled the start of federal measures to control monopolistic activity. This act, along with later laws such as the Clayton Act and the founding of the Federal Trade Commission (FTC), provided the framework for today's antitrust rules, which have expanded their reach to a variety of sectors including real estate. Antitrust laws have a special impact on the real estate market, influencing how professionals conduct business to maintain fairness and competitiveness.

Prohibited Practices
1. **Price-Fixing**: An agreement among competitors to set prices for services or products rather than letting the market dictate pricing is illegal. In real estate, this could manifest as brokers agreeing on standard commission rates.
2. **Market Allocation**: Agreements among competitors to divide markets by geographical area or type of transaction are prohibited. Such practices prevent consumers from benefiting from competition.
3. **Group Boycotting**: When two or more businesses conspire to prevent another business from competing in the market, it constitutes a group boycott, which is illegal.
4. **Tie-In Arrangements**: It is illegal to force customers to purchase an unwanted product or service in exchange for a desired one. In real estate, this might involve requiring buyers to use a specific lender or title company.

Noncompliance with antitrust rules can result in serious penalties such as fines, legal action, and harm to one's professional reputation. Real estate professionals must operate transparently, with an emphasis on fair competition and client service.

The enforcement and adherence to antitrust regulations in the real estate sector are critical to guaranteeing a fair and competitive market. Several major institutions, most notably the Federal Trade Commission (FTC) and the Department of Justice (DOJ), are responsible for implementing these rules by actively monitoring and investigating industry practices to prevent anti-competitive behavior. The Federal Trade Commission and the Department of Justice play critical roles in antitrust enforcement. They examine real estate company agreements, investigate allegations of anti-competitive behavior, and take legal action against firms that violate these regulations. Their operations are intended to prohibit acts that may affect customers by limiting choices or unfairly raising costs.

Strategies for Compliance

For real estate professionals, maintaining compliance with antitrust laws is not only a legal necessity but also a testament to their commitment to ethical practices. Strategies for ensuring compliance include:

- **Regular Training**: Professionals should engage in ongoing education regarding antitrust laws to stay informed about legal standards and prohibited practices. This education can help prevent inadvertent violations and foster a culture of compliance.
- **Legal Consultation**: Consulting with legal experts who specialize in real estate and antitrust law can provide valuable guidance, especially when navigating complex transactions or agreements that may raise antitrust concerns.
- **Adherence to Ethical Guidelines**: Many real estate organizations and associations offer ethical guidelines that align with antitrust laws. Adhering to these guidelines not only supports legal compliance but also enhances the profession's integrity.

Antitrust laws are essential for maintaining a competitive, fair, and vibrant real estate market. The FTC and DOJ's persistent enforcement of these rules, together with real estate professionals' proactive compliance efforts, helps to safeguard consumers, preserve market integrity, and encourage healthy competition. As the real estate market evolves, so will the application and interpretation of antitrust laws, mandating ongoing vigilance and dedication to ethical business practices from all industry players.

CHAPTER 11: FUNDAMENTAL CALCULATIONS IN REAL ESTATE

BASIC REAL ESTATE MATH AND PRACTICAL APPLICATIONS

Mathematical proficiency is essential in the real estate market, since it serves as the foundation for a wide range of transactions and analysis. Math is a vital instrument that provides precision and reliability in all aspects of real estate business, from first property value assessments to the detailed calculations required in finalizing a purchase.

Mathematical skills enable real estate professionals to undertake detailed property analysis, make accurate financial assessments, and carry out deals with confidence. Whether establishing a property's fair market value, calculating loan interest rates, or estimating investment returns, mathematical acumen ensures that professionals navigate the complexity of the real estate market with competence and honesty.

Real estate professionals encounter a variety of calculations on a daily basis, including but not limited to:

- Determining property areas and volumes for valuation purposes.
- Calculating commission rates for real estate transactions.
- Assessing loan amounts, interest rates, and mortgage payments.
- Estimating taxes, insurance premiums, and investment returns.

These calculations are critical for giving correct information to clients, making informed investment decisions, and guaranteeing the smooth completion of real estate transactions.

Conversions in Real Estate

Conversion formulas are essential when dealing with properties in different measurement units. One of the most common conversions in real estate involves transforming square footage into acres for land valuation.

Conversion Formula: Acres = Square Feet/43,560
Example: To convert a 10,000 square foot lot into acres: (10,000 sq ft) x (1 acre/43,560 sq ft) = 0.229 acres

Decimals, Percentages, and Fractions

The use of decimals, percentages, and fractions is prevalent in real estate calculations, particularly in determining financial metrics such as interest rates, commission rates, and prorations. These ideas are critical for effectively evaluating the costs and rewards on real estate deals.

Interest Rate Calculations:

For simple interest calculations: Interest = Principal x Rate x Time

For a loan of $100,000 at an annual interest rate of 5% over 5 years: $100,000 x 0.05 x 5 = $25,000

Commission Rate Calculations:

Commission is often calculated as a percentage of the sale price: Commission = Sale Price x Commission Rate

For a $500,000 sale with a 6% commission rate: $500,000 x 0.06 = $30,000

Prorations:

Prorations divide expenses between buyer and seller based on how long each party will own the property during the billing term: Prorated Amount = (Annual Cost/365) x Days of Responsibility

For property taxes of $3,650 paid by the seller up to the sale date, 120 days into the year: ($3,650/365) x 120 = $1,200

Financial Mathematics in Real Estate

Understanding financial mathematics is crucial for investment analysis and mortgage calculations.

Capitalization Rate (Cap Rate): A measure of real estate investment return.

Cap Rate = Net Operating Income (NOI)/Property Value

For a property valued at $1,000,000 generating $100,000 NOI: Cap Rate = $100,000/$1,000,000 = 10%

Loan-to-Value (LTV) Ratio: A metric used by lenders to assess the risk of a mortgage loan.

LTV = (Loan Amount/Property Value) x 100%

For a $800,000 loan on a $1,000,000 property: LTV = ($800,000/$1,000,000) x 100% = 80%

FINANCIL ANALYSIS WITH T-BAR METHOD

The T-BAR Method is an important technique in the real estate industry, notably for analyzing property investments. This method uses a simple graphical representation to analyze the financial performance of real estate properties, focusing on income, expenses, and cash flow. Understanding and utilizing the T-BAR Method enables investors, real estate brokers, and financial analysts to make sound decisions about property investments. At its foundation, the T-BAR Method is a visual tool for simplifying financial analysis of real estate assets. It depicts income and expenses as two opposing bars on a graph, with the difference indicating the net cash flow from the property.

The T-BAR Method is useful for a number of reasons. It offers a clear, rapid visual picture of a property's financial performance, allowing for quick assessments and comparisons. By simplifying complex financial data, stakeholders can properly assess the viability and profitability of property projects.

Components of the T-BAR Method

1. Top Bar - Income Streams: The top bar of the T-BAR graph represents the property's various income streams. This could include:

- Rental income from tenants
- Fees for parking facilities
- Income from vending machines or laundry facilities within the property
- Any other consistent revenue generated by the property

Understanding the composition and reliability of these income streams is vital for assessing the property's financial health.

2. Bottom Bar - Expenses and Liabilities: The lower bar of the T-BAR details the property's recurring expenses and liabilities, which might encompass:

- Mortgage payments or loan interest
- Property taxes and insurance premiums
- Maintenance and repair costs
- Utility expenses if not passed on to tenants
- Management fees

Accurately calculating these expenses is essential for a realistic assessment of the property's net cash flow.

3. Net Cash Flow: Net cash flow is calculated by subtracting total expenses (bottom bar) from total income (top bar). This figure shows the property's real financial return, indicating its profitability and investment possibilities.

Using the T-BAR Method: A Step-by-Step Guide

To employ the T-BAR Method effectively, envision creating a simple "T" shaped diagram, either on paper or digitally, where the horizontal lines represent the income and the vertical line of the "T" represents the expenses associated with a property.

Creating the T-BAR Diagram

1. **Start with a Blank Sheet**: Whether using pen and paper or a digital spreadsheet, begin by drawing a large "T" on the page.
2. **Scale for the Bars**: The length of each bar (both income and expenses) should be proportional to the amounts they represent. For instance, you might decide that every inch (or centimeter) on your diagram represents $1,000. If your annual rental income is $12,000, the income bar would be 12 inches (or centimeters) long if using this scale.
3. **Marking Income and Expenses**: On the top bar, mark the various sources of income, extending the bar to match the total income according to your scale. Do the same for expenses on the bottom bar, ensuring each expense is accounted for and the total length reflects the sum of all expenses.
4. **Calculating Net Cash Flow**: Once both bars are drawn, visually comparing their lengths will give you an immediate sense of the property's financial performance. If the income bar is longer, the difference between the two bars represents your net cash flow. Conversely, if the expenses bar is longer, it indicates a negative cash flow.

The key to the T-BAR Method's efficacy is the proportional depiction of financial statistics. Before drawing, select a scale that reflects the financial magnitude of your property investment. This scale converts abstract figures into practical visual comparisons, allowing you to analyze the property's profitability at a glance.

The T-BAR Method simplifies financial analysis in real estate, providing a simple way to illustrate a property's income vs expenses, and thus its profitability. Real estate specialists may quickly and effectively evaluate investment prospects by converting financial data into proportionate bars on a simple diagram, making this method a useful tool for anybody interested in understanding the financial complexities of property investing.

CALCULATIONS RELATED TO MORTGAGES, TAXES, AND VALUATIONS

The mathematics of mortgages is critical for both real estate professionals and clients. It entails knowing how loans are arranged to finance real estate purchases, including principle, interest rates, and the loan's amortization plan.

- **Principal**: This is the original loan amount used to finance the property acquisition. It is the base figure upon which interest is calculated.
- **Interest Rate**: Represented as a percentage, the interest rate is charged on the outstanding principal and is the lender's fee for borrowing the loan amount.
- **Amortization**: This refers to the practice of spreading out the loan (principal and interest) over a set number of years, ending in full payback at the end of the period.

Calculating monthly payments is an important component of mortgage math since it requires a specific formula to determine how much a borrower must pay each month toward principal and interest. The formula is given by:

Monthly Payment = $P\{r(1+r)^n\}/\{(1+r)^n-1\}$

Where:
- P is the principal loan amount.
- r is the monthly interest rate, derived from the annual interest rate divided by 12.
- n is the total number of payments, calculated as the loan term in years multiplied by 12 (for months).

Example: Consider a $200,000 mortgage at a 5% annual interest rate, set on a 30-year term. First, convert the annual interest rate to a monthly rate $0.05/12 = 0.004167$ and identify the total number of payments $30 \times 12 = 360$. Plugging these figures into the formula calculates the monthly payment.

Impact of Down Payments

The quantity of a down payment has a major impact on the total loan amount and, consequently, monthly mortgage payments. A larger down payment reduces the loan amount required to purchase the home, resulting in reduced monthly payments and total interest paid throughout the loan's life.

- A substantial down payment effectively lowers the loan-to-value ratio, potentially qualifying the borrower for better loan terms and interest rates.
- Additionally, putting down 20% or more can avoid the necessity for private mortgage insurance (PMI), a common requirement for loans with higher loan-to-value ratios.

Example: On a $250,000 property, a 20% down payment would be $50,000, reducing the mortgage needed to $200,000. The down payment not only affects the initial loan amount but also influences the borrower's monthly financial commitment and the total interest cost over the life of the loan.

By mastering these aspects of mortgage calculations, real estate professionals can guide clients through the complexities of financing a property purchase, ensuring informed decisions that align with their financial capabilities and goals.

Property Tax Calculations

Property tax computations are an important part of real estate transactions, influencing both buyers and sellers. Understanding these computations allows experts to appropriately calculate the annual financial burdens that come with property ownership.

Local governments apply property taxes calculated on the property's estimated value. These taxes pay a variety of public services, including schools, highways, and emergency services. The local tax assessor determines the assessed value, which may not necessarily be the same as the property's market value.

The formula to calculate annual property taxes is straightforward:

Annual Property Tax = Assessed Value x Tax Rate
Assessed Value: The dollar value assigned to a property to measure applicable taxes, determined by the local tax assessor.
Tax Rate: Usually expressed as a percentage or mill rate (one thousandth of a dollar), set by the local government.

For instance, if a property's assessed value is $200,000 and the local tax rate is 1.25%, the annual property tax will be computed as follows:

$200,000 x 0.0125 = $2,500

This calculation informs homeowners of their annual property tax liability, crucial for budgeting purposes.

Prorations in Real Estate Transactions

Prorations of property taxes are typical at closing, ensuring that both the buyer and seller pay their respective parts of the annual property taxes based on the amount of time each party owns the property throughout the tax year. Prorations are calculated according to the closure date. For example, if a property sale occurs halfway through the tax year, the seller is responsible for property taxes until the closing date, while the buyer is responsible for the rest of the year. The proration formula is:

Prorated Tax = \textAnnual Property Tax (Number of Days Seller Owned Property/365)

If the annual property tax is $2,500 and the seller owned the property for 182 days before closing, the seller's prorated tax responsibility would be:

$2,500 x (182/365) = $1,250

These computations guarantee an equitable distribution of property tax responsibilities between the buyer and seller at the moment of sale.

In real estate, it is critical to accurately calculate and comprehend property taxes. Real estate professionals must be skilled in determining and explaining property tax responsibilities, whether they are planning a new home purchase or closing a sale. This experience guarantees that clients are aware of their annual financial obligations and facilitates the seamless implementation of real estate transactions.

Real Estate Valuations

In real estate, precise valuation is critical, influencing everything from listing pricing to property taxes and investment appraisals. Valuation procedures provide the tools required to determine a property's value in a competitive market. Let's look at the fundamental principles and processes that support real estate valuations.

Property valuation encompasses several key concepts essential for understanding a property's worth:

- **Market Value**: The most probable price a property would command in a competitive and open market.
- **Assessed Value**: A public tax assessor assigns a value to a property for tax reasons.
- **Appraised Value**: An objective expert's assessment of a property's value at a given moment.

Understanding these different values is critical for real estate professionals to navigate transactions, assess property taxes, and guide investment decisions.

Capitalization Rate Calculation

For investment properties, the capitalization rate (cap rate) is an important metric that calculates the return on investment and indicates the property's prospective profitability. The cap rate is calculated using the following formula:

Cap Rate = Net Operating Income (NOI)/Property Value

Net Operating Income (NOI): The annual income earned by the property after deducting operational costs but before mortgage payments and taxes.

Property Value: The actual market value of the property.

For example, a property with an NOI of $50,000 and valued at $500,000 would have a cap rate of:

Cap Rate = $50,000/$500,000 = 0.10 or 10%

A higher cap rate indicates a larger return on investment, making it an important indicator for investors evaluating property prospects.

Real estate valuation is a complex yet critical component of the industry, necessitating a thorough understanding of market dynamics and financial research. Real estate experts who know the art of property valuation, such as CMAs and cap rate calculations, can ensure correct pricing, enhance investment returns, and instill buyer and seller confidence. As the market evolves, maintaining current on valuation trends and methodology will remain a key component of successful real estate practice.

CALCULATING THE DECREASE IN PROPERTY VALUE

Understanding the subtleties of property value drop is critical in today's dynamic real estate landscape. This decline has the potential to severely affect a variety of stakeholders, including homeowners, investors, and real estate professionals, altering decision-making and financial planning.

The term "decrease in property value" refers to a drop in the worth or market value of real estate property over time. While real estate often appreciates, various factors might cause a drop, affecting profitability, return on investment, and marketability.

Several factors can precipitate a decrease in property value, each intertwining with broader market dynamics and individual property characteristics:

1. **Market Fluctuations**: The real estate market is susceptible to cycles of boom and bust, influenced by national and global economic conditions. A market downturn can cause broad decreases in property values.
2. **Neighborhood Decline**: Changes in a neighborhood, such as increased crime rates or declining public services, can deter potential buyers, leading to decreased property values.
3. **Property Condition Deterioration**: Lack of maintenance or neglect can lead to physical deterioration, reducing a property's appeal and value.
4. **Economic Factors**: Economic downturns, rising unemployment rates, and interest rate hikes can decrease demand for property, leading to lower values.

Understanding these factors is crucial for real estate professionals to navigate the complexities of the market, advise clients accurately, and develop strategies for mitigating the impact of a decrease in property value.

Methods for Calculating Decrease in Property Value

When dealing with a drop in property value, it is critical to use several analytical tools to accurately analyze and quantify the decline. While we've previously covered Comparative Market Analysis (CMA) as a method for analyzing current market values, it's important to note that CMA may also be used to compare current values to historical data to identify property value reductions. This approach, coupled with the Cost Method and the Income Approach, forms a comprehensive framework for understanding and assessing value depreciation.

1. Comparative Market Analysis (CMA): As previously stated, a CMA is an effective tool for property appraisal since it compares a subject property to similar properties that have recently sold in the region. When focusing on the reduction in property value, CMAs might reveal market trends and shifts that are not immediately evident. Real estate professionals can uncover patterns of value drop by monitoring comparative sales over time, which they can then attribute to larger market dynamics or individual property difficulties.

2. Cost Method: Repair and Renovation Analysis: The Cost Method delves into the financial implications of bringing a property up to its optimum marketable condition. This approach calculates the decrease in property value by:

- *Assessing Physical Condition*: Conducting a thorough inspection to determine any necessary repairs and modifications.
- *Estimating Repair Costs*: Obtaining quotes and estimates for all work required to restore the property to a desirable condition.
- *Calculating Depreciation*: Subtracting the total cost of repairs and renovations from the property's current market value, derived from a CMA, to determine the decreased value.

This method is particularly useful for properties that have suffered from neglect or require significant updates, providing a tangible figure for the decrease in value due to physical deterioration.

3. Income Approach: Evaluating Reduced Income Potential: For investment properties, the Income Approach is a critical method for calculating the decrease in property value based on reduced income potential. This approach involves:

Determining Net Operating Income (NOI): Calculating the property's potential income after accounting for all operating expenses.

Assessing Income Reductions: Identifying factors that could lead to decreased NOI, such as higher vacancy rates, increased maintenance costs, or market-driven rent reductions.

Applying Cap Rate: The capitalization rate is used to calculate a property's amount based on its income-generating ability, with lower NOI signifying a drop in value.

This method provides a direct correlation between a property's income-generating ability and its market value, highlighting how decreases in potential income directly impact overall valuation.

MEASUREMENTS

In the real estate industry, measurement accuracy can have a substantial impact on many aspects of property transactions, from the first listing to the final sale and legal documents. Accurate measures are not only essential for fair dealings, but they also play a key role in property valuation, impacting decisions made by buyers, sellers, and investors alike. Accurate measurements are required to facilitate transparent, equitable, and legally sound real estate transactions. They contribute to property descriptions, aid in valuation, and are necessary for zoning and property development planning. Measurement discrepancies can cause arguments, affect property values, and potentially derail deals.

Real estate professionals utilize several units of measurement, each appropriate for different aspects of property and land assessment:

- **Square Feet (sq ft) and Square Meters (sq m)**: Primarily used for the interior measurement of buildings and rooms, providing a clear picture of the usable space.
- **Acres and Hectares**: Commonly used for measuring larger land parcels. An acre is used in the imperial system, while a hectare is part of the metric system, with 1 hectare equaling 10,000 square meters.

The accurate measurement of land is crucial for determining property boundaries, calculating sale prices, and planning development projects.

Surveying Basics

Land surveying is the measurement and charting of land boundaries and features. To create precise land descriptions, surveyors employ a variety of equipment, including traditional transit and tape measurements as well as modern GPS and laser scanning technologies. This process is critical for determining property boundaries, settling disputes, and assuring compliance with municipal zoning requirements.

Calculating the area of land parcels is essential for understanding the size and value of a property. The basic formulas used include:

- Rectangle or Square: Length x Width
- Triangle: (Base x Height) / 2

These calculations aid in determining lot size, which contributes to property valuation and allows for easier comparisons. For irregularly shaped parcels, more complicated geometric computations or surveyor interventions may be required. Surveyors may use complicated geometric computations to break down irregularly shaped parcels into simpler shapes like triangles and rectangles. After computing the area of each component form, the total area of the parcel is determined by adding the individual areas. This method offers a more precise representation of the land's overall size. Furthermore, Geographic Information Systems (GIS) and Computer-Aided Design (CAD) software play an important role in dealing with irregular parcels since they can process spatial data and generate detailed maps and diagrams of land.

House Measurements

Accurate house measurements are critical in real estate, influencing everything from property listings to appraisals and legal documents. Let's look at the differences between exterior and interior measures, how to accurately measure rooms and spaces, and how these measurements affect property listings.

1. Exterior Measurements are taken from the outside walls of a house and are typically used to calculate the total footprint or gross external area of the property. These measurements are important for:

- **Determining Lot Coverage**: Assessing how much of the property is covered by the building, which is crucial for zoning and development regulations.
- **Initial Valuation Estimates**: Providing a quick method to estimate property size before detailed interior measurements are taken.

2. Interior Measurements focus on the livable or usable space within the house, excluding the thickness of external walls. They are critical for:

- **Listing and Marketing Properties**: Accurate interior measurements ensure that listings reflect the true usable space, a key factor for buyers.
- **Appraisals and Comparisons**: Appraisers and real estate professionals use interior measurements to compare properties and determine market value.

Measuring individual rooms and spaces requires precision and attention to detail. Here are some criteria for precise measurements:

- **Use a Consistent Method**: Whether using a laser measure, tape measure, or another device, consistency is key. Always measure from wall to wall at the widest points.
- Account for Built-ins and Non-livable Spaces: Ensure to note any built-in features, such as cabinets or fireplaces, that may affect the usability of the space. Non-livable spaces, like closets or utility areas, should be measured but listed separately from the livable square footage.
- **Document Everything**: Keep detailed records of measurements for each room, including any irregularities or unique features. This documentation can be invaluable for creating floor plans or marketing materials.

Accurate house measurements significantly influence property listings and the marketing process:

Buyer Perceptions: Listings that accurately reflect the size and layout of a home can positively impact buyer perceptions, making a property more attractive and potentially speeding up the sale process.

Valuation Accuracy: Correct measurements ensure that valuations are based on precise data, leading to fair pricing and preventing disputes during the sale process.

Marketing Material Quality: High-quality, accurate measurements allow for the creation of detailed floor plans and other marketing materials, enhancing the listing's appeal to prospective buyers.

CHAPTER 12 – EXAM SIMULATION

Welcome to the thorough exam simulation chapter, which will test your knowledge and prepare you for the rigors of the real estate license exam. This simulation covers a variety of real estate-related issues, including property regulations, ethical standards, financial computations, and much more. Through a sequence of carefully constructed multiple-choice questions, you'll be able to apply what you've studied in a style that is similar to the actual exam. Whether you're a seasoned professional looking to refresh your abilities or a beginner looking to break into the business, this simulation is an excellent tool for self-assessment and revision. As you progress, try to think about each question carefully, using both your knowledge and thinking to choose the best answer. Good luck!

1. Which of the following best describes the role of a 'Grantor'?
A) Receives property rights
B) Transfers property ownership
C) Manages property rentals
D) Funds real estate projects

2. What distinguishes Planned Unit Developments (PUDs) from other types of common interest developments?
A) They do not include shared ownership of common areas.
B) They exclusively feature commercial spaces.
C) Owners have individual title to their homes and a shared interest in common areas.
D) They are primarily designed for agricultural use.

3. Which valuation method is especially relevant for income-producing properties?
A) Cost Approach
B) Sales Comparison Approach
C) Income Capitalization Approach
D) Replacement Cost Method

4. Which of the following best describes the 'bundle of rights' associated with real property ownership?
A) The rights to use, rent, or destroy the property only.
B) The rights to use, exclude others, dispose of, and enjoy the property.
C) The rights to access the property for specific purposes.
D) The rights to change zoning laws applicable to the property.

5. A real estate contract that does not clearly state the purpose and is against public policy is lacking in:
A) Legality
B) Offer
C) Acceptance
D) Consideration

6. Which sort of deed offers the buyer the greatest amount of protection, ensuring clear title?
A) Quitclaim deed
B) Warranty deed
C) Special warranty deed
D) Trust deed

7. Which type of deed offers the highest level of buyer protection by guaranteeing against any title problems?
A) Quitclaim Deed
B) Bargain and Sale Deed
C) General Warranty Deed
D) Special Warranty Deed

8. Which formula represents the calculation for annual property taxes?
A) Annual Property Tax = Tax Rate + Assessed Value
B) Annual Property Tax = Assessed Value x Tax Rate
C) Annual Property Tax = Assessed Value / Tax Rate
D) Annual Property Tax = Tax Rate / Assessed Value

9. For what purpose are escrow accounts also used, besides holding down payments in real estate transactions?
A) Paying the real estate agent's commissions
B) Managing ongoing expenses related to the property
C) Investing in property upgrades before the sale
D) Covering moving expenses for the buyer

10. Which types of leases require the tenant to pay not only rent but also some or all of the property's expenses, like insurance, taxes, and maintenance?
A) Gross Lease
B) Modified Gross Lease
C) Net Lease
D) Percentage Lease

11. Which is NOT a recognized risk in property leasing and management?
A) Physical damage to the property
B) Decreased property value due to market trends
C) Liability issues from accidents
D) The popularity of nearby restaurants

12. Which type of agency agreement provides an agent with the exclusive right to market and sell a property?
A) Open Listing
B) Exclusive Agency
C) Exclusive Right to Sell
D) Non-Exclusive Buyer Agency Agreement

13. Which real estate contract grants a buyer the right, but not the obligation, to buy a property for a certain price within a specific timeframe?
A) Option Contract
B) Exclusive Right to Sell Contract
C) Buyer Agency Agreement
D) Open Listing Contract

14. Which lease type is most common in retail, especially malls and shopping centers?
A) Ground Lease
B) Percentage Lease
C) Net Lease
D) Gross Lease

15. A 'Cure or Quit Notice' is typically issued for:
A) Non-payment of rent
B) Violation of lease terms other than rent payment
C) Completion of a property sale
D) Notification of property maintenance issues

16. What is title insurance designed to protect homeowners and lenders against?
A) Natural disasters impacting the property
B) Future property tax increases
C) Losses arising from defects in the title
D) Physical damages to the property post-purchase

17. Which type of title insurance policy is typically required by mortgage lenders?
A) Owner's Policy
B) Lender's Policy
C) General Policy
D) Enhanced Policy

18. Which law was enacted in part to combat practices like blockbusting and steering in real estate?
A) The Affordable Care Act
B) The Fair Housing Act of 1968
C) The Consumer Protection Act
D) The Equal Pay Act

19. What is the impact of not making a 20% down payment on a mortgage?
A) Reduction in property taxes
B) Increase in the interest rate
C) Requirement to pay private mortgage insurance (PMI)
D) Automatic denial of the mortgage application

20. Which method is commonly used to handle irregularly shaped land parcels during surveying?
A) Breaking down the parcel into simpler shapes for area calculations
B) Estimating the area based on neighboring property sizes
C) Using the color of the land as a guide
D) Consulting a lawyer

21. What is the first step in establishing an escrow account for a real estate transaction?
A) Paying the full property price to the escrow agent
B) Selection of a neutral third party to act as the escrow agent
C) Signing the final sale agreement
D) Conducting a property appraisal

22. Which party is NOT typically protected by an escrow account in a real estate transaction?
A) Buyer
B) Seller
C) Lender
D) Neighbor

23. State and local fair housing laws:
A) Replace the need for the Fair Housing Act
B) Can provide broader protections than federal laws
C) Are only applicable to commercial properties
D) Decrease the number of protected classes

24. In the context of real estate contracts, the 'Sale of Existing Home' contingency allows the buyer to:
A) Increase the offer price based on the sale of their current home.
B) Withdraw from the purchase if they sell their current home for less than expected.
C) Proceed with the acquisition only if they can sell their current property.
D) Request a reduction in the sale price if their current home sells quickly.

25. A buyer's agent is primarily responsible for:

A) Listing properties on behalf of the seller.

B) Finding and negotiating the purchase of a property on behalf of the buyer.

C) Managing rental properties for a landlord.

D) Conducting home inspections.

26. Interest-only mortgages allow borrowers to:

A) Skip mortgage payments for the first year

B) Pay only the interest portion for a set period

C) Avoid paying property taxes

D) Pay off the mortgage in half the time

27. Economic trends influence the real estate market through:

A) Changes in local sports team rankings

B) Variations in celebrity endorsements of properties

C) GDP growth rates and unemployment levels

D) Seasonal weather patterns

28. What does the Income Capitalization Approach primarily focus on?

A) The architectural design of the property

B) The historical significance of the property

C) The net income the property is expected to generate

D) The color scheme of interior design

29. How are adjustable-rate mortgages (ARMs) different from fixed-rate mortgages?

A) Interest rates on ARMs fluctuate over time in response to market conditions.

B) ARMs require a larger down payment.

C) Fixed-rate mortgages are only for commercial properties.

D) ARMs are interest-free loans.

30. The Equal Credit Opportunity Act (ECOA) prohibits credit discrimination based on:

A) Loan amount requested

B) The type of property being purchased

C) The borrower's income source

D) The borrower's color, race, religion, sex, national origin, age, marital status or receipt of public assistance

31. Which types of loans surpass the conforming lending restrictions established by Freddie Mac and Fannie Mae?

A) Adjustable-rate mortgage

B) FHA loan

C) Jumbo loan

D) VA loan

32. What is the main purpose of conducting a Comparative Market Analysis (CMA)?

A) To determine the highest possible price for a property regardless of market conditions

B) To establish a fair market value by comparing the property to similar ones recently sold

C) To calculate the annual property taxes

D) To decide on the color and design of a property before listing

33. Accessibility regulations in building codes aim to:

A) Increase property values

B) Make buildings navigable for people with disabilities

C) Limit the height of buildings

D) Promote energy efficiency

34. Which of the following is NOT considered an effective method of notification in real estate transactions?

A) Direct verbal communication in a public setting.

B) Written notices delivered by mail.

C) Electronic communication via email.

D) Official documents shared through online platforms.

35. Which of the following best describes the principle of 'Loyalty' under fiduciary duties?

A) Ensuring the property is listed on all major websites.

B) Acting in the best interests of the client above all others.

C) Keeping all communication in writing.

D) Ensuring timely payment of property taxes.

36. Which element ensures that all parties involved in a contract are of legal age and sound mind?

A) Legality

B) Mutual Assent

C) Capacity

D) Offer and Acceptance

37. Which type of eviction notice is issued for non-payment of rent?

A) Cure or Quit Notice

B) Pay Rent or Quit Notice

C) Unconditional Quit Notice

D) Notice of Lease Termination

38. Which deed provides no warranties about the property's title?

A) General Warranty Deed

B) Special Warranty Deed

C) Quitclaim Deed

D) Grant Deed

39. For a deed to be considered valid, it must NOT include:
A) The legal capacity of the parties
B) A detailed description of the property
C) A declared intent to convey property
D) The current market value of the property

40. What does a General Warranty Deed guarantee to the buyer?
A) The property has no physical damages.
B) The seller has not previously sold the property to someone else.
C) There will be no future increases in property taxes.
D) The buyer is protected against any title problems that might arise.

41. In the T-BAR Method of financial analysis, the bottom bar represents:
A) Property income
B) Expenses and liabilities
C) The height of the building
D) The length of the property

42. The calculation of prorated property taxes at closing ensures:
A) That the buyer pays for all renovations
B) An equitable distribution of tax liability based on ownership time
C) The seller receives a bonus
D) The real estate agent receives a higher commission

43. A 'cloud on title' refers to:
A) A temporary legal protection against property sale
B) The geographical location of a property
C) Any irregularity or dispute that affects the title's clarity
D) The environmental impact assessment of a property

44. What type of commercial lease typically includes the landlord paying most of the property's operating expenses?
A) Triple Net Lease
B) Gross Lease
C) Percentage Lease
D) Variable Lease

45. Under the Uniform Electronic Transactions Act (UETA), what legal standing do electronic signatures have?
A) No legal standing unless printed and signed manually.
B) Limited legal standing for non-financial transactions.
C) The same legal standing as handwritten signatures.
D) Recognized only for internal corporate communications.

46. What is NOT a typical component of a Purchase Agreement in real estate?
A) Buyer's credit score
B) Property details
C) Sale price and payment terms
D) Contingencies, such as inspections

47. Real estate professionals violate their legal responsibilities when they:
A) Advocate for the best interests of their clients.
B) Use confidential information for their client's advantage.
C) Fail to disclose known defects in a property to potential buyers.
D) Negotiate the best possible price for their client.

48. What is the essence of an agency relationship in real estate?
A) An agreement where a property is leased for a short period.
B) A legal agreement allowing an agent to act on behalf of a client in transactions.
C) A contractual relationship solely for property maintenance.
D) A temporary partnership for property development.

49. What role does a guarantor play in the real estate financing process?
A) Guarantees construction quality
B) Ensures the property taxes are prepaid
C) Commits to fulfilling the loan obligations if the borrower defaults
D) Acts as a witness during the signing of the mortgage

50. What does a mortgage primarily represent in real estate financing?
A) A legal agreement to rent property
B) A type of insurance policy for home repairs
C) A loan specifically designed for the purchase of real estate
D) An agreement between real estate agents

51. Eminent domain allows the government to:
A) Change zoning laws at will
B) Take private property for public use with fair compensation
C) Sell public lands to the highest bidder
D) Override building codes for infrastructure projects

52. What is the primary characteristic of a cooperative (Co-op) in real estate?

A) Owners have direct ownership of their individual units.

B) Ownership is based on shares in a corporation that owns the property.

C) It is a type of investment property with no shared ownership in common areas.

D) Each owner has an undivided interest in the property.

53. Which of the following is a focus of building codes?

A) Determining property tax rates

B) Regulating stock exchanges

C) Ensuring structural integrity and safety

D) Designing urban landscapes

54. Who are the primary certification bodies mentioned for real estate licensing exams?

A) National Association of Realtors (NAR) and American Real Estate Society (ARES)

B) PSI and Pearson VUE

C) Federal Real Estate Administration (FREA) and National Testing Network (NTN)

D) American Society of Real Estate Agents (ASREA) and Global Real Estate Institute (GREI)

55. Which form of joint ownership includes the right of survivorship?

A) Tenancy in Common

B) Sole Proprietorship

C) Joint Tenancy with Right of Survivorship (JTWROS)

D) Limited Liability Company (LLC)

56. Private Mortgage Insurance (PMI) is required when:

A) The down payment is less than 20% of the home's purchase price

B) The borrower chooses a fixed-rate mortgage

C) The property is located in a rural area

D) The loan is a jumbo loan

57. Which practice is prohibited under the Equal Credit Opportunity Act (ECOA)?

A) Charging interest on loans.

B) Discriminating against applicants on the basis of age or marital status.

C) Requiring a credit check for loan approval.

D) Refusing to lend to individuals without a steady income.

58. What type of real estate contract is primarily used to outline the terms under which a tenant occupies a property?

A) Financing Contract

B) Lease Agreement

C) Purchase Agreement

D) Listing Agreement

59. What is the primary purpose of notification in real estate transactions?

A) To finalize the sale without the need for further discussion.

B) To communicate offers, counteroffers, and amendments to contract terms.

C) To publicly announce the sale of a property.

D) To declare the agent's commission rates.

60. What is a critical practice for dispute avoidance in real estate transactions?

A) Limiting communication with the other party to written form only.

B) Making all decisions unilaterally without consulting the other party.

C) Clear and transparent communication throughout the transaction process.

D) Using high-pressure tactics to speed up the negotiation process.

61. Which of the following is NOT a protected class under the Fair Housing Act?

A) Marital status

B) National origin

C) Religion

D) Disability

62. What signifies legal ownership and the right to use the property in real estate transactions?

A) A mortgage

B) A title

C) A lease agreement

D) An inspection report

63. Which of the following is true about the delivery and acceptance of a deed?

A) Delivery is optional if the deed is signed

B) Acceptance by the grantee is presumed if the transfer benefits them

C) Delivery and acceptance can only occur in the presence of a judge

D) Acceptance is valid only if accompanied by a monetary transaction

64. What is a key feature of a Special Warranty Deed?

A) It guarantees the property is free from liens.

B) It covers the property's entire history.

C) It only covers the period during which the seller owned the property.

D) It transfers personal property only.

65. Why is the neutrality of the escrow agent crucial in real estate transactions?

A) To ensure the property is legally owned by the agent

B) To maintain impartiality and act in the best interest of both parties

C) Because the escrow agent is responsible for property maintenance

D) To determine the final selling price of the property

66. How does a larger down payment affect a mortgage?

A) Increases the total interest paid over the life of the loan

B) Decreases the monthly mortgage payments

C) Has no effect on the mortgage terms

D) Shortens the amortization period automatically

67. What does the practice of "blockbusting" typically involve in the real estate industry?

A) Encouraging homeowners to invest in property improvements

B) Promoting the use of green energy in homes

C) Inducing property sales by exploiting fears of neighborhood decline

D) Offering free home evaluations to all potential sellers

68. Which of the following is NOT a typical responsibility of an escrow agent in a real estate transaction?

A) Holding the buyer's down payment

B) Ensuring the property is insured

C) Managing the documents related to the property transfer

D) Conducting the final property inspection

69. What must a valid deed include to ensure it accurately identifies the property being transferred?

A) The original construction date of the property

B) An adequate property description

C) The future development plans for the area

D) The previous sale price of the property

70. What does a deed in a real estate transaction represent?

A) The legal right to use the property

B) A physical document transferring property ownership

C) A contract for property maintenance services

D) The tenant's agreement to pay rent

71. What must landlords do with a tenant's property left behind after an eviction?

A) Dispose of it immediately

B) Return it to the tenant without charge

C) Store it for a specific period allowing the tenant to claim it

D) Sell it immediately to cover unpaid rent

72. What does a modified gross lease offer to tenants and landlords?

A) A fixed rent that includes all property expenses

B) Rent adjustments based on the tenant's revenue

C) Flexibility in how expenses are allocated between the tenant and landlord

D) The tenant pays all property-related expenses

73. In the context of leasing and property management, what does the Fair Housing Act prohibit?

A) Renting properties over a certain price

B) Discrimination based on disability

C) Leasing properties to individuals under 30

D) Renting out properties for less than six months

74. What is a primary benefit of utilizing electronic transactions in real estate, as facilitated by UETA?

A) Elimination of the need for inspections and appraisals.

B) Speeding up the transaction process with quick document sharing and signing.

C) Completely removing the need for real estate agents.

D) Guaranteeing a higher sale price for properties.

75. A Special Warranty Deed guarantees against title defects:

A) Only during the specific period the seller owned the property

B) Throughout the property's entire history

C) Only before the seller acquired the property

D) None of the above

76. Why is recording the deed an essential step in finalizing the transfer of real estate?

A) It updates the property's physical condition.

B) It confirms the property's market value.

C) It gives public notice of the new ownership.

D) It revises the property's zoning status.

77. What is NOT a direct benefit of escrow accounts for lenders in real estate transactions?

A) Ensuring property taxes and insurance premiums are paid on time

B) Guaranteeing a higher interest rate on the mortgage

C) Safeguarding the value of the property serving as collateral

D) Protecting the lender's interest in the property

78. The capitalization rate in real estate is used to:

A) Determine the property's color scheme

B) Calculate the property's return on investment

C) Measure the physical size of the property

D) Assess the property's landscaping value

79. Which of the following is a primary advantage of using an escrow account for buyers in a real estate transaction?

A) It reduces the property price.

B) It eliminates the need for property insurance.

C) It provides a layer of security by holding the down payment.

D) It speeds up the property appraisal process.

80. What is a primary benefit of using the T-BAR Method in real estate investment analysis?

A) It simplifies property design choices

B) Provides a clear visual representation of financial performance

C) It calculates the exact number of tiles needed for roofing

D) Determines the best interior decorators for a property

81. Calculating the commission on a $500,000 sale with a 6% commission rate would result in:

A) $3,000

B) $30,000

C) $300

D) $300,000

82. What is a primary difference between an enhanced and a standard title insurance policy?

A) Enhanced policies only cover commercial properties.

B) Standard policies do not protect against fraud.

C) Enhanced policies offer broader coverage for specific risks.

D) Standard policies are renewable annually.

83. Which statement accurately describes a Grant Deed?

A) It guarantees no prior conveyance of the property

B) It is mainly used to convey personal property

C) It offers the same level of protection as a Quitclaim Deed

D) It cannot be used in residential property transactions

84. Which of the following best describes a marketable title?

A) A title with no public record

B) A title that carries the highest interest rate

C) A title free from serious legal questions or disputes

D) A title exclusively for commercial properties

85. In real estate, 'title' refers to:

A) The name of a property's legal document

B) A property's listing status on the market

C) The legal right to own, use, and dispose of property

D) The blueprint and design specifications of a building

86. What is a primary responsibility of a property manager?

A) Negotiating property sales

B) Screening potential tenants

C) Designing properties

D) Conducting public auctions

87. Which dispute resolution method is characterized by a neutral third party facilitating negotiation between disputing parties?

A) Arbitration

B) Mediation

C) Litigation

D) Conciliation

88. The process of ensuring a property can be transferred with a clear title involves:

A) Obtaining a new property insurance policy

B) Renovating the property before sale

C) Conducting a comprehensive title search and resolving any disputes

D) Increasing the property's curb appeal

89. What does the execution of the deed officially convey in a real estate transaction?

A) The buyer's mortgage approval

B) The property from the seller to the buyer

C) The real estate agent's commission

D) The closing date and time

90. What is "steering" in the context of real estate transactions?

A) Guiding clients to make sustainable housing choices

B) Directing buyers to or away from certain neighborhoods based on discrimination

C) Navigating clients through the home buying process with expert advice

D) Encouraging clients to steer clear of fixed-rate mortgages

91. What is the primary purpose of the Fair Housing Act established in 1968?

A) To regulate the mortgage lending industry

B) To ensure equal access to rental and housing opportunities

C) To govern the sale prices of residential properties

D) To standardize the construction of residential buildings

92. What legal document specifies the conditions under which a renter is allowed to inhabit a property?

A) A mortgage agreement

B) A construction permit

C) A lease agreement

D) A deed of sale

93. In a real estate transaction, what term is used to describe the monetary value traded as part of the contract?

A) Dividend

B) Bonus

C) Consideration

D) Incentive

94. The Truth in Lending Act (TILA) requires lenders to:

A) Provide borrowers with details about loan costs and terms

B) Approve all loan applications

C) Offer the lowest possible interest rate

D) Grant loans without a credit check

95. What does the 'Right of First Refusal' contractual clause provide a party in a real estate transaction?

A) The first opportunity to lease the property before it's offered to others.

B) The first chance to purchase the property at a predetermined price.

C) The ability to refuse any offers made on the property first.

D) Priority to refuse to pay the commission if unsatisfied with the service.

96. Which of the following is considered an antitrust violation in real estate?

A) Offering competitive commission rates

B) Brokers agreeing on standard commission rates

C) Marketing a property on various platforms

D) Providing accurate property valuations

97. Under what condition can landlords typically issue an 'Unconditional Quit Notice'?

A) Late rent payment

B) A minor lease violation

C) Repeated lease violations or significant damage to property

D) Tenant requests early lease termination

98. What is a Financing Contingency clause primarily concerned with?

A) Ensuring the buyer renovates the property post-purchase.

B) Guaranteeing the seller finds a new home before selling.

C) Allowing the buyer to exit the contract if financing isn't secured.

D) Protecting the agent's commission in case of buyer default.

99. The Fair Credit Reporting Act (FCRA) is important in real estate because it:

A) Sets the interest rates for mortgages.

B) Regulates the collection and use of consumer credit information.

C) Determines the commission rates for real estate agents.

D) Defines the legal descriptions of properties.

100. A high Debt-to-Income Ratio (DTI) indicates that a borrower:

A) Has an excellent credit score

B) Owns multiple properties

C) May struggle to manage monthly payments

D) Is employed in the real estate industry

Question n.	Answer	Question n.	Answer
1	B) Transfers property ownership	51	B) Take private property for public use with fair compensation
2	C) Owners have individual title to their homes and a shared interest in common areas	52	B) Ownership is based on shares in a corporation that owns the property
3	C) Income Capitalization Approach	53	C) Ensuring structural integrity and safety
4	B) The rights to use, exclude others, dispose of, and enjoy the property	54	B) PSI and Pearson VUE
5	A) Legality	55	C) Joint Tenancy with Right of Survivorship (JTWROS)
6	B) Warranty deed	56	A) The down payment is less than 20% of the home's purchase price
7	C) General Warranty Deed	57	B) Discriminating against applicants on the basis of age or marital status
8	B) Annual Property Tax = Assessed Value x Tax Rate	58	B) Lease Agreement
9	B) Managing ongoing expenses related to the property	59	B) To communicate offers, counteroffers, and amendments to contract terms
10	C) Net Lease	60	C) Clear and transparent communication throughout the transaction process
11	D) The popularity of nearby restaurants	61	A) Marital status
12	C) Exclusive Right to Sell	62	B) A title
13	A) Option Contract	63	B) Acceptance by the grantee is presumed if the transfer benefits them
14	B) Percentage Lease	64	C) It only covers the period during which the seller owned the property
15	B) Violation of lease terms other than rent payment	65	B) To maintain impartiality and act in the best interest of both parties
16	C) Losses arising from defects in the title	66	B) Decreases the monthly mortgage payments
17	B) Lender's Policy	67	C) Inducing property sales by exploiting fears of neighborhood decline
18	B) The Fair Housing Act of 1968	68	D) Conducting the final property inspection
19	C) Requirement to pay private mortgage insurance (PMI)	69	B) An adequate property description
20	A) Breaking down the parcel into simpler shapes for area calculations	70	B) A physical document transferring property ownership

21	B) Selection of a neutral third party to act as the escrow agent	71	C) Store it for a specific period allowing the tenant to claim it
22	D) Neighbor	72	C) Flexibility in how expenses are allocated between the tenant and landlord
23	B) Can provide broader protections than federal laws	73	B) Discrimination based on disability
24	C) Proceed with the acquisition only if they can sell their current property.	74	B) Speeding up the transaction process with quick document sharing and signing
25	B) Finding and negotiating the purchase of a property on behalf of the buyer.	75	A) Only during the specific period the seller owned the property
26	B) Pay only the interest portion for a set period	76	C) It gives public notice of the new ownership
27	C) GDP growth rates and unemployment levels	77	B) Guaranteeing a higher interest rate on the mortgage
28	C) The net income the property is expected to generate	78	B) Calculate the property's return on investment
29	A) Interest rates on ARMs fluctuate over time in response to market conditions.	79	C) It provides a layer of security by holding the down payment
30	D) The borrower's color, race, religion, sex, national origin, age, marital status or receipt of public assistance	80	B) Provides a clear visual representation of financial performance
31	C) Jumbo loan	81	B) $30,000
32	B) To establish a fair market value by comparing the property to similar ones recently sold	82	C) Enhanced policies offer broader coverage for specific risks
33	B) Make buildings navigable for people with disabilities	83	A) It guarantees no prior conveyance of the property
34	A) Direct verbal communication in a public setting	84	C) A title free from serious legal questions or disputes
35	B) Acting in the best interests of the client above all others	85	C) The legal right to own, use, and dispose of property
36	C) Capacity	86	B) Screening potential tenants
37	B) Pay Rent or Quit Notice	87	B) Mediation
38	C) Quitclaim Deed	88	C) Conducting a comprehensive title search and resolving any disputes
39	D) The current market value of the property	89	B) The property from the seller to the buyer
40	D) The buyer is protected against any title problems that might arise	90	B) Directing buyers to or away from certain neighborhoods based on discrimination
41	B) Expenses and liabilities	91	B) To ensure equal access to rental and housing opportunities

42	B) An equitable distribution of tax liability based on ownership time	92	C) A lease agreement
43	C) Any irregularity or dispute that affects the title's clarity	93	C) Consideration
44	B) Gross Lease	94	A) Provide borrowers with details about loan costs and terms
45	C) The same legal standing as handwritten signatures	95	B) The first chance to purchase the property at a predetermined price
46	A) Buyer's credit score	96	B) Brokers agreeing on standard commission rates
47	C) Fail to disclose known defects in a property to potential buyers	97	C) Repeated lease violations or significant damage to property
48	B) A legal agreement allowing an agent to act on behalf of a client in transactions.	98	C) Allowing the buyer to exit the contract if financing isn't secured
49	C) Commits to fulfilling the loan obligations if the borrower defaults	99	B) Regulates the collection and use of consumer credit information
50	C) A loan specifically designed for the purchase of real estate	100	C) May struggle to manage monthly payments

CHAPTER 13 - NEXT STEPS: STARTING YOUR CAREER

TIPS FOR EARLY SUCCESS IN THE FIELD

In navigating the competitive and intricate terrain of the real estate industry, prospective professionals frequently seek a road map for early success. Achieving distinction in this sector involves more than just a basic understanding of laws and regulations; it also necessitates a deliberate approach to career development, client relations, and continual learning. This chapter digs into practical guidance for those looking to make their mark in the real estate industry, laying out a road to not only success, but also greatness and leadership within the profession.

1. **Strategic Networking and Mentorship**: Success in real estate is heavily reliant on the networks that professionals form and the mentors they engage. Networking, which is frequently misunderstood as ordinary socializing, is in fact a strategic undertaking. It entails discovering and cultivating relationships with people from all aspects of the real estate market, from experienced brokers and agents to clients, developers, and legal professionals. Each link provides new insights and opportunities, allowing professionals to improve their knowledge and increase their market presence. Engaging a mentor is also crucial. An experienced expert can offer vital insights into negotiating market problems, creating client connections, and making sound business decisions. The National Association of Realtors (NAR), through initiatives such as the Realtor Mentorship Program, provides structured opportunities for newbies to learn from experienced professionals, demonstrating the industry's understanding of mentorship's importance.

2. **Client-Centric Approaches**: The key to real estate success is developing and keeping strong client connections. This starts with a thorough grasp of the clients' wants and goals, whether they're purchasing their first house or investing in commercial property. Real estate agents must thrive at communication by demonstrating empathy, transparency, and responsiveness. The Real Estate Settlement Procedures Act (RESPA) emphasizes the significance of honest dealings by outlawing bribes and unearned fees and requiring clients to receive complete information about all transactions. Furthermore, client ties go beyond specific transactions. A successful real estate professional sees each client engagement as the start of a long-term

relationship, punctuated by regular check-ins and the sharing of key market insights. This technique not only fosters loyalty, but it also generates referrals, which are a crucial driver of business growth.

3. **Technological Proficiency and Innovation**: In an era where technology is altering every sector, real estate professionals must be skilled at using digital technologies. Technology improves efficiency and client interaction in a variety of ways, including online listings and virtual tours, as well as CRM systems. The epidemic has expedited the digital shift, with sites such as Zillow and Redfin gaining popularity for their complete online offerings. Real estate agents that can traverse these platforms and incorporate them into their marketing and sales strategies are ahead of the competition. Furthermore, technology advancements present opportunities for real estate professionals to distinguish themselves. For example, using drones for aerial property photography or implementing blockchain technology for secure, transparent transactions both demonstrate a forward-thinking approach that appeals to clients and distinguishes a professional from competition.

4. **Legal and Ethical Integrity**: A successful real estate career is built on strict adherence to legal norms and ethical ideals. This requires a detailed awareness of applicable legislation, ranging from the Fair Housing Act, which forbids discrimination in housing transactions, to state-specific licensing requirements. Professionals must stay up to date on legislative changes by taking continuing education classes and attending industry seminars. In contrast, ethical integrity is adhering to the ideals of fairness, honesty, and respect in all interactions. The NAR Code of Ethics, for example, specifies responsibilities to clients, the public, and fellow Realtors, providing a thorough framework for ethical behavior. Adherence to these principles not only assures regulatory compliance, but also fosters confidence among clients and coworkers, a valuable asset in the real estate market.

5. **Market Analysis and Continuous Learning**: A thorough understanding of market dynamics allows real estate professionals to provide useful insights to clients, helping them through challenging decisions with confidence. This necessitates not only an understanding of current trends and prices, but also the capacity to forecast future market moves. Professionals can accomplish this by conducting thorough analyses of market data, economic indicators, and municipal development goals. Continuous learning is essential for keeping this market competence. The real estate sector is always evolving, with new trends, legislation, and technology appearing on a regular basis. Participating in professional development opportunities, whether through formal schooling or industry conferences, ensures that real estate professionals remain at the forefront of their sector, ready to give first-rate service to their clients.

To summarize, early success in real estate is the outcome of planned, informed initiatives, rather than chance. By creating genuine connections, addressing client requirements, embracing technology, adhering to legal and ethical standards, and committing to continual learning, prospective real estate professionals can lay the framework for a rewarding and distinguished career. Real estate success is both demanding and rewarding, with chances to make a long-term difference in the lives of customers and the community as a whole.

CONCLUSION

As we come to the end of our "Real Estate License Exam Prep," it's important to take a moment to reflect on what we've learned. From the complex laws governing property transactions to the ethical considerations that underpin professional conduct, from the mathematical calculations that form the foundation of valuations and mortgages to the strategies that ensure antitrust compliance, this guide has been designed to provide you with the knowledge and skills you need to succeed in the real estate industry.

More than just a collection of data and figures, this book aims to create in you a sense of confidence and preparation. Real estate is a field full with prospects, but it demands a high level of professionalism and attention. The next exam is more than simply a memory test; it is also a measure of your readiness to begin a profession that influences communities and changes lives.

As you embark on this exciting new phase, keep in mind that diligence, integrity, and an unshakable commitment to study are the keys to success in both the exam and your future job. The real estate landscape is always shifting, with new challenges and possibilities arising at every step. However, with the foundation you've laid via your education, you're well prepared to navigate these waters.

Take this opportunity to recognize the effort you've put into your preparations. To get here, I had to cultivate patience, tenacity, and a growth attitude, in addition to learning new things. These traits can help you navigate the complexities of the real estate industry and carve out a successful, meaningful career.

As you approach the exam, be certain that you have covered all of the bases and will pass on your first try. Trust the preparation you've done, the knowledge you've learned, and the insights you've gained from each chapter of this guide. Approach each question calmly and clearly, confident in your ability to apply what you've learned in a practical, intelligent way.

Finally, let this book serve as both a tribute to what you've learned and a light of what's to come. The route for becoming a licensed real estate professional is fraught with opportunities. You are prepared to make a lasting effect on the real estate industry because you are armed with information, guided by ethics, and motivated by a desire to make a difference. Best wishes on achieving this milestone, and best of luck as you take this critical step toward achieving your professional objectives. The future seems promising, and it awaits your input!

GLOSSARY

Welcome to the Glossary chapter of our book. Here, you will find a curated selection of the most frequently used terms in the realm of real estate. These important concepts serve as the foundation for understanding how to successfully manage the complexities of real estate transactions, regulations, and principles.

1. **Adjustable-Rate Mortgage (ARM)**: A mortgage with variable interest rate that varies according to market conditions.
2. **Amortization**: The procedure of spreading out a loan in a series of predetermined payments over time.
3. **Appraisal**: A certified specialist provides an estimate of a property's market worth.
4. **Assessment**: The valuation of property for tax purposes.
5. **Balloon Mortgage**: A mortgage with low monthly payments and a large final payment.
6. **Broker**: A person authorized to negotiate and organize real estate transactions.
7. **Building Codes**: Regulations that set the standards for construction and safety of buildings.
8. **Buyer's Agent**: A real estate agent who represents the buyer in a property transaction.
9. **Capital Gains Tax**: Profits from the sale or investment of property are subject to taxation.
10. **Closing**: The last stage in completing the acquisition of a property.
11. **Closing Costs**: Taxes incurred at the end of a real estate transaction.
12. **Commission**: A fee paid to a real estate agent for services rendered.
13. **Comparative Market Analysis (CMA)**: An analysis used to estimate a home's value based on the sales of similar properties.

14. **Condominium (Condo)**: A private residence within a larger building or complex.
15. **Contingency**: A provision in a real estate contract that requires a specific condition to be met.
16. **Deed**: A legal document that transfers ownership of property.
17. **Depreciation**: A decrease in the value of property over time.
18. **Down Payment**: An initial payment made when purchasing a property.
19. **Earnest Money**: A deposit paid to a seller to demonstrate the buyer's good faith in a deal.
20. **Easement**: A permission to cross or utilize someone else's territory for a specific purpose.
21. **Equity**: The variation between a property's market value and the amount due.
22. **Escrow**: A financial agreement where an outside party keeps and controls the payment of funds needed by two parties involved in a certain transaction.
23. **Fair Housing Act**: U.S. legislation that prohibits discrimination in buying, selling, renting, or financing of housing.
24. **Fixed-Rate Mortgage**: A mortgage having a consistent interest rate throughout the duration of the loan.
25. **Foreclosure**: The process by which a lender seizes control of a property due to failure to make mortgage payments.
26. **FSBO (For Sale By Owner)**: Property that is sold by the owner without the assistance of a real estate agent.
27. **Homeowners Association (HOA)**: An organization in a planned community, subdivision or condominium that develops and enforces rules for the properties under its control.
28. **Home Inspection**: An examination of a property's condition, usually conducted by a qualified inspector.
29. **Lease**: A contract by which one party transfers property to another for an established interval of time, typically in exchange for a periodic payment.
30. **Lien**: A legal right or interest that a lender has in the property of another until a debt is paid off.
31. **Listing**: A property that is available for sale.
32. **Market Value**: The price at which a property would sell under current market conditions.
33. **Mortgage**: A loan used to purchase a property.
34. **Mortgage Broker**: An individual or corporation who connects borrowers and lenders to assist them assure a mortgage loan.
35. **Multiple Listing Service (MLS)**: A database created by participating real estate brokers to give details about properties for sale.
36. **Offer**: A official proposition to purchase a property at a specific price.
37. **Pre-approval**: A lender's conditional agreement to lend a specified amount to a borrower before they choose a home.
38. **Pre-qualification**: An informal assessment by a lender of the amount a borrower may qualify to borrow.
39. **Principal**: The sum of money borrowed on a loan, or the balance owed on a mortgage, minus interest.
40. **Property Management**: Real estate and physical property management includes control, maintenance, operations and oversight.
41. **Real Estate Agent**: A person authorized to negotiate and carry out real estate deals.
42. **Real Estate Broker**: A person who has completed additional study beyond the agent level and passed the broker's licensing exam.
43. **Refinancing**: Obtaining a new mortgage to replace an original agreement.
44. **Title**: Legal documentation proving ownership of property.
45. **Title Insurance**: Insurance that protects the holder against loss caused by faults in the title.
46. **Title Search**: A search of the public records to establish that the seller is the legitimate proprietor of the real estate and that no liens or other claims exist.
47. **Underwriting**: The procedure by which a lender determines the risk of lending funds to a homebuyer.
48. **VA Loan**: A mortgage loan in the United States backed by the Department of Veterans Affairs.
49. **Warranty Deed**: A deed that ensures a clear title to the buyer of real estate.
50. **Zoning**: Regulations governing how properties in specific geographic zones may be used.

Made in United States
Troutdale, OR
10/15/2024

23771240R00064